STEALING HOME: A CON'S GUIDE TO INHERITANCE THEFT

EDITION 2

STEALING HOME

A Con's Guide To Inheritance Theft
Edition 2

Phillip C. Lemmons, Esq.

DEDICATION

This book is dedicated to seniors suffering from abuse at the hands of cons disguised as family members.

ACKNOWLEDGMENTS

My heartfelt thanks go to the following people for helping me stay focused. Without their support and encouragement, this project would have gone into extra innings.

To my wife Pamela, for keeping the wheels oiled.
To my children, for teaching me to balance work and play.
To my mother Bonnie, for modeling unconditional love.
To my extended family members, for their willingness to help.
To my friends and colleagues, for their various contributions, especially: Nancy Gomez Tamayo, Charlene Tran, Jennifer Wright, Dan Hoppy, David Chon, Mickee Williams and Tracy Stevenson.

CONTENTS

GETTING STARTED

"In theory there's no difference between theory and prac-
tice. In practice there is." ~ Yogi Berra

CROWD CHATTER FADED AS A masterful rendition of The Star
Spangled Banner graced the stadium. Team managers and players
stood side-by-side conforming to baseball chivalry. Hundreds of
broadcasters sat mic ready in the mezzanine. The World Series pre-
game activities were unfolding according to plan. Then Dan Dignitary
climbed the pitcher's mound for the ceremonial first pitch. With an
exaggerated arm windmill warm up, he reached back to throw. As
his momentum carried forward, he lost balance and stumbled to the
ground. It was a classic first pitch folly, witnessed by millions on live
television. Dan is not the only dignitary to make that mistake. There
are highlight reels full of first pitch follies. With so much at stake, why
don't dignitaries practice throwing from a pitcher's mound before the
game?

Dignitaries enjoy high rank or office. Their opinions influence our lives. They are busy, self-reliant, hard-working and confident. They also know how to get things done. They expect to win, and the more they win the more they underestimate challenges. Why would anyone like that take the time to practice something as ordinary as throwing a baseball?

Be prudent in safeguarding your inheritance. Don't be a Dan Dignitary. At least recognize it can be stolen. Cons are determined to take your parents' life savings, and they are everywhere. They are family members, loyal friends, trusted neighbors, business partners and professionals. They are also perfect strangers. Since they can be anyone, they are invisible. Cons are good at hiding their intentions too. They strike quickly, and with precision. One might be targeting one of your family members right now.

It's not easy discussing inheritance theft with your parents. It assumes their demise, makes you appear greedy and presumptuous, and may even open old wounds. Most people remain silent until something happens. They let cons strike first.

I am going to help you handle this delicate situation. You'll learn how cons target seniors, pick their methods and carry-out scams. You'll be armed with tools to detect, deter and defend against inheritance theft.

INTRODUCTION

A LOS ANGELES MAN NAMED Jeff called requesting a minute of my time. His upbeat greeting was quickly replaced by sadness. People have difficultly masking their feelings, especially when fighting pain. He explained that his mother had recently lost a battle with pancreatic cancer. While offering my condolences, he gently interrupted. "Thank you, but that's not why I called. It's about my father." I remained quiet and started taking notes. "My Dad was grieving Mom's passing when my sister Ruth moved into his house. Since she was between jobs and Dad enjoyed having family nearby, it seemed like a great idea." Her trust motives were unthinkable. We'll get to that later.

"Dad and I played golf ever Saturday for the past six years. I routinely picked him up at 6 am. Last Saturday I knocked for several minutes before Ruth answered the door. She cracked it open and in a cold and distant tone of voice told me to leave. I asked for Dad, and while closing the door she said, 'He died last Monday.' She wouldn't let me in to talk, so I rushed home and made several attempts to contact her by phone. She returned my calls earlier today. She was rude and refused to discuss Dad's death. Instead, she claimed to have authority over all his matters as agent of his power of attorney. I didn't even know Dad had a power of attorney. She said we are skipping the funeral because Dad wanted to be buried at sea. I tried changing her mind but, she said Dad's cremated remains were with the Neptune Society."

Jeff briefly paused before cutting loose in an angry rant. "Why is Ruth doing this to me? Why didn't she call when Dad died? Why won't she tell me what happened? Why didn't she talk to me about his funeral? Why is she treating me like a stranger? He's my father too. Is she allowed to do that?"

Jeff was trying to rationalize his sister's absurd behavior. He even started questioning his own judgment. He just couldn't accept the obvious. Ruth is a ruthless con. When people hide the passing of a parent, make unilateral decisions, seize control and refuse to communicate with immediate family members, they are taking that parent's assets. They are cons! "There is probably a lot more to this story," I explained. "Ruth may have already taken, or is in the process of taking all of your father's assets. She probably started planning it months ago and wants to finish before you catch on. She is savvy. The longer she keeps you away, the more she will take. And, don't be surprised if her name appears on the deed to your father's house."

Jeff interrupted. "Are you saying that I just lost my family and my inheritance?"

"Probably, yes," I explained. "I'm sorry."

My firm gets a steady stream of phone calls from people just like

Jeff. Close family members start drifting apart after the death of a parent. For no apparent reason the person in charge of their parent's estate or trust becomes rude, short-tempered and disrespectful. They view the assets as their own and reject their fiduciary duties to be fair and impartial. They replace the parent's wishes with their own. They acknowledge family members that submit to their authority and punished those that don't. They, threaten to deplete estate and trust assets by hiring expensive probate litigators to defend their actions. They make people like Jeff feel hopeless.

In theory, parents direct the post-death distribution of their assets by will or trust. In practice, those decisions are sometimes changed by cons. The number of cons raiding assets owned by infirm seniors and their estates and trusts is growing. Government agencies are trying to help through legislation and enforcement, but they can't prevent inheritance theft. Stopping Cons is especially tough because they can operate overtly in the face of unsuspecting family members. I wrote this book to curb inheritance theft, so let's get started.

Understanding some trust and estate terminology will help improve communication. Don't worry. Memorizing an entire lexicon of legalese is not necessary. Just familiarize yourself with the following terms. They used throughout this book.

Benefactors and Beneficiaries

Benefactors are people that make bequests or endowments. They give their assets to beneficiaries. Beneficiaries are the recipients of those gifts. For example, if you receive $25,000 from your father's trust, he is a benefactor because he gave away the money and you are a beneficiary because you benefited from the gift. Benefactors are not always parents though. They can be other family members, distant relatives, close friends or even charities. They can be any person or legal entity. Beneficiaries can also be any person, charity or other legal entity.

Cons and Marks

Cons are people that scam benefactors by fraud, force, deceit or confidence tricks. They are also known as con men and con artists. Most people think cons are shifty, suspicious looking characters with beady eyes and handle-bar mustaches. They are not. Cons don't look like cons. They look like your banker, hair stylist, neighbor, or brother. They look like you and me.

Inheritance Theft Explained

Inheritance theft is the wrongful taking of assets from benefactors or their estates or trusts. It's a relatively new term, one you won't find in a dictionary—at least not yet. The literal phrase "inheritance theft" is a misnomer because an inheritance is a right that can't be stolen. Cons aren't interested in your right to inherit, however. They want the objects of those rights. They want your benefactor's assets.

Assets can be transferred from one generation to the next in many different ways. They change hands via wills, trusts, payment on death accounts, financial account beneficiary designations, title designations, life-time gifts, and so on. Cons can manipulate those instruments through or around an infirm benefactor. They forge signatures and employ confidence scams, manipulation and coercion to get what they want. The best Cons use more than one method of transferring assets to maximize their take.

The objects of your anticipated inheritance may include a house, automobiles, intellectual property rights, collectibles, and money. They are not considered part of your actual inheritance until a legal right to receive them has vested. Until then, they belong to the benefactor or their estate or trust. So, why do we refer to the wrongful taking of your benefactor's assets inheritance theft? We do because theft from a benefactor or their estates or trusts has an immediate, substantial and direct effect on the object of your natural inheritance. That is to say, as your benefactor loses assets to cons the value of your anticipated inheritance decreases.

Cons follow common methods of operation. What separates them is the skill in which they execute their scams. Ruth's scam included redirection and speed. While Jeff spent time searching for answers about his father's death, Ruth loaded up the assets. She acted swiftly, taking as much as possible before anyone could stop her. There are "Ruth's" in every family. They are physically undetectable, and they might even throw you off by their pleasant personality or close relationship. But, their actions may give them away. Recognizing common methods of operation could lead to early detection and prevention. Here are the ten most common methods used today:

Ten Common Methods of Operation

1. Cons use authority as successor trustees to steal assets directly from the benefactor's family trust.
2. Cons trick or pressure benefactors into signing grant deeds that give them a joint tenancy interest in a home. (If the joint tenancy deed is properly executed and recorded, ownership of the home will automatically go

to the con upon the benefactor's death. To clear title, the con need only record an affidavit of death of joint tenant.)

3. Cons create living trusts in a benefactor name for their benefit—as the sole or primary beneficiary. They then trick or pressure a benefactor into signing the trust. Once the trust is signed, they legally transfer the assets to themselves.

4. Cons amend a benefactor's family trust, for their benefit—as the sole or primary beneficiary. They trick or pressure a benefactor into signing the amendment. Then they legally transfer the assets to themselves.

5. Cons create distress stories designed to trick or pressure a benefactor into periodically giving them money.

6. Cons induce benefactors, by trickery or pressure, into making them the 100% beneficiary of the benefactor's savings account by signing a beneficiary designation card. Upon the benefactor's death, everything in the account privately transfers to the con.

7. Cons use agency authority under a benefactor's power of attorney to directly deposit money from the benefactor's investment, retirement, and social security benefits into their personal bank accounts.

8. Cons raid a recently deceased benefactor's house, taking hard to recover valuables such as coin collections, precious metals, art, photographs, stamps, jewelry and other family heirlooms.

9. Cons use fraud, duress, undue influence, or forgery to make a will or trust that names them as the 100% beneficiary of a benefactor's assets.

10. Cons use their authority as a conservator to misappropriate money from the conservatee's (benefactor's) estate.

Prevention Is Key

States legislatures are passing new laws to protect benefactors from financial scams and abuses. They are also revising old laws to make the apprehension and prosecution of cons easier. Although that may lead to the arrest of more cons, government agencies will never replace stolen assets. They could even impose huge fines, but most cons are not deterred by threats of financial penalties; some hide their assets, seldom pay taxes and usually have a number of creditors chasing them down. They take pride in beating the system. Courts can order them to return stolen assets, but unless they follow orders (somewhat unlikely), or you can locate and freeze their assets (also unlikely), the orders will remain unenforceable. That's why it's so important for you to focus on inheritance theft prevention. If you ever suspect a con is targeting your benefactor, get help from a trust and estate litigation attorney right away.

Pre-Game Speech

Chinese General Sun-Tzs once said, "The best victory is when your opponent quits of his own accord before there are any actual hostilities." He knew that engaging in war would result in some harm even if his army was victorious. Winning emotionally charged legal battles excites attorneys and clients alike, but courtroom victories are expensive. The estate of J. Howard Marshall paid millions in legal fees to defend against Anna Nicole Smith's somewhat absurd claims. Yet, sitting on your hands while a con raids your benefactor's assets may cost more. There is a happy medium between doing nothing and full blown litigation. Beneficiaries that acknowledge inheritance theft risks and take preemptive action can deter cons. They can achieve the best victory.

The remaining chapters are written in satire—cons are the fictional audience in a training seminar. As the reader your perspective changes to a fly-on-the-wall as cons are taught how to commit inheritance theft. Hopefully the birds-eye view will help you learn to think like a con, and protect your parents from their scams.

✳ ✳ ✳

Case Notes

'57 CHEVY DOWN 66

EMILY SKIPPED THE SMALL TALK. She gave her name and cut straight to the point. "My brother stole my inheritance! He stole my inheritance! Can you believe it?" A stolen inheritance is not new to me, but her word choice caught my attention. Callers that visit us at www.thelegacylawyers.com use buzzwords like "stolen inheritance." I knew immediately she was part of our team--one of our cherished visitors who keep a close eye on their inheritance rights by reading our newsletters and blog posts, and watch our videos.

Emily spoke quickly, breathlessly running sentences together. "I love my big brother. He's everything to me. I love his wife and kids. Our children play together. We eat supper together every Sunday. I can't believe he scammed us like that. We're family." As she went on, I quickly took notes, recording key facts as they poured out. Her words seem to melt together, revealing an obvious southern dialect.

"What's your brother's name?" I asked.

"It's Lee. He's my oldest brother, the first born. I have a younger brother, too. His name is Travis, and he's still 'n Texas. I followed Lee out here after the accident. When Daddy was in the hospital, Lee promised to take care of us. We trusted him with everything. Now he claims the assets 'n Daddy's trust were used to pay medical bills. I know that's a lie. They were fully insured. My parents promised that everything 'n the trust would be divided equally between us kids. They would turn in their graves if they knew Lee took it all for himself. Can you help?"

Emily asked the ultimate question and wanted a straightforward answer. She wasn't in the mood for uncommitted attorney talk about jurisdiction, client identification, conflicts checks and case theories. She wanted help, and she wanted it now. I couldn't answer her question without additional information, so I quickly asked, "Where does Lee live now?"

"He's here 'n California," she said. It was clear that court jurisdiction could rest in California. But before I could ask another question, she went back to her story. "They were both killed in a car accident. Momma died at the scene, but Daddy lived for two more days. They hit head-on into an eighteen-wheeler on old Route 66."

"Did they live in Texas at the time of the accident?" I asked.

"Yes," she said. "They loved driving Daddy's '57 Chevy down 66."

Still unsure about my legal theory, I pressed on. "Did your parents have a will or trust?"

"Yes. Yes, they had a trust, but Lee has it now. He has their power of attorney too. He has all of it--he's 'n charge. We all moved here over a year ago, except for Travis. He stayed home in Texas."

It appeared that Lee breached his duties as trustee of the trust, but I needed more information, and fast. Similar to a homicide investigation, it's crucial to quickly gather information at the beginning of a case. I needed copies of the will, trust, powers of attorney, bank and brokerage statements, life insurance policies, asset inventories, titles, deeds, business agreements, and tax returns. I needed the names of all possible witnesses, doctors, and lawyers. Having Lee's personal and financial information would also be helpful. I needed one more thing. I needed her brother Travis to join us. Probate court judges usually rule more favorably for beneficiaries that stand together in unity.

We set an appointment for the next morning. Emily's quick reaction was impressive. Most beneficiaries in her situation are paralyzed by denial. They wait, foolishly hoping for the best. Not Emily. She wasn't going to be cheated. As a member of our team, she knew better than to wait and hope. She took the bull by the horns. If a judge finds that Lee breached his duties, he will replace Lee with another trustee. Furthermore, because of Emily's swift action, all stolen assets will likely be recovered at Lee's expense.

STEP 1

CHAPTER ONE

DOES STEALING HOME MAKE SENSE?

"The future ain't what it used to be." ~ *Yogi Berra*

ARE YOU READY TO MAKE real money? I am talking about hundreds of thousands of dollars, and without a lifetime of hard work, saving, and financially prudent behavior. Interested? Well, buckle-up because I am going to show you how to do it in six easy steps. These steps are similar in approach to those used by baseball players attempting to steal home. Oh, I know you are not professional athletes. Don't worry—baseball just helps with the big picture. Natural talent isn't necessary either. Getting rich using my techniques is easy if you follow the steps in this book. I guarantee you'll never have to work for someone else again.

Stealing home is one of the most dramatic plays in baseball. Some fans think it is more exciting than a game-winning, walk-off home run. The 1955 photo of Jackie Robinson stealing home just under Yogi Berra's tag is a baseball treasure. In the early days of baseball, base runners had a better chance of stealing home because pitchers were lagging in their ability to prevent them from taking big leads. That has changed today. Instead of throwing from a windup when runners are on third base, pitchers use a shortened motion called a stretch. Now, holding runners close to third base is much easier. That minor adjustment has resulted in far fewer attempts at stealing home because the risk of getting caught is much higher.

As a savvy con, you are like a base runner in the early days of baseball, and your mark's beneficiary is the pitcher. You currently have the advantage. Like pitchers in the early days, beneficiaries are lagging in their ability to stop you. Most don't even know about the game. Since catching them by surprise is the key to your success, you need to get going. Start by evaluating your risk tolerance. There's no mathematical formula, just ask yourself these questions: Does stealing home make sense? Is the timing right? Do you stand to inherit anything from your mark? If so, how much would you get by waiting and doing nothing? Is your mark infirm? Do you have influence over her? Is she well protected? Is she isolated from family and friends? How much are you willing to risk? The next two chapters will help you determine if acting now makes sense.

CHAPTER TWO

FIVE REASONS TO COMMIT INHERITANCE THEFT

YOU MAY HAVE MIXED FEELINGS about stealing from a mark because the action is inconsistent with your values. Psychologists refer to this as cognitive dissonance. It occurs when your actions and thoughts conflict with each other. Stealing is immoral, but if you need the money to pay a gambling debt or risk a broken leg, you might also think it's acceptable. Don't worry. Those emotions can be managed by minimizing the negative effect on your self-image. The conflict can be reconciled—and your self-image preserved—if your actions are justified. To ease tensions associated with scamming your mark, simply look for justifications. These five are commonly used:

Addictions Are Expensive

Feeding your addiction requires sacrificing vacations, reliable transportation, new clothes, hobbies, and even healthy foods. It's not your fault you were genetically inclined to take drugs, shop excessively, play the horses, or sip an afternoon martini. Nobody knows how terrible you feel, nor do they care. They don't understand the loneliness, the pain behind your forced smiles, your failed relationships or your constant run-ins with police. They don't know what it's like to be fired every couple of months or to spend more time with strangers in group therapy than with family around the dinner table. So forget them! Start enjoying the fullness of your life, addiction and all.

You Were Dealt a Bad Hand

Some say you have to play the hand you're dealt. I think the people who say that were dealt great hands. It's not your fault that mom was diagnosed with cancer when you were five, or that your father couldn't earn enough to feed the family, or your single mother lost everything in an apartment fire. Does your bad hand affect you more personally? Were you wrongfully convicted of a crime? Do you suffer from ADHD or a developmental disorder? Were you born with an aggressive personality? Did you grow up in a dysfunctional home? Were your parents' drug addicts, neglectful, or abusive?

It's not on you. Those conditions were not the consequences of poor choices. You were just unlucky. Wouldn't it be nice if you could simply get another hand? How would you like another chance to live the good life? Well, you no longer have to settle for the hand you were dealt, throw it away and draw more cards.

You're Entitled

You were born different from everyone else; you're unique. Let others work for a living, sacrifice for down-payments, and wear last year's fashions. You have rights. Your parents should have recognized that years ago. You deserved a new Mercedes-Benz SLR McLaren at 16, just like Paris Hilton. You were right to indulge in the latest fashions during college, because your parents had some making up to do. It's time everyone started treating you like a princess. You should be the boss with a corner office, even though you lack work experience. You have the right to quit your job and collect unemployment benefits if co-workers don't make you happy. You deserve luxurious accommodations wherever you go. You should use credit cards to support your high standards. Your parents can help pay the bill, even if their share is all of it. If they refuse, discharge your debts through bankruptcy. You're entitled to the best that life has to offer, and you only live once, so live to the fullest.

Putting It To Better Use

Is your mark mismanaging his wealth? Does he fail to see the value of an aggressive investment strategy? Is his standard of living too high? Are assets being wasted on meaningless cruises or lavish senior living facilities? Wouldn't that money be better used on your new home, or paying off your debts, or to fund your new business venture? When it's too difficult to stand by and watch the value of your inheritance slowly decrease because of poor financial decisions, take control. Remember, you are doing this to help your mark (wink, wink). Hurry because if you don't step up now, he could lose it all before dying.

Honoring Your Parents

Children honor their parents through obedience. Adults do it by respect. You can show respect for your parents by visiting, helping with difficult tasks, and making sure their medical needs are being met. You can do it for a mentally incapacitated or deceased mother by continuing her legacy. Take control of her funeral services, seize her belongings, and redirect her mail to your address. Let everyone know you are in charge, even if you lack the legal authority to act. If her will or trust doesn't "accurately" reflect her final wishes, then make it right. Follow your instincts when distributing assets. Don't be afraid to give yourself more than everyone else. After all, you are taking time from your busy schedule to help. Be firm with beneficiaries who interfere. Ignore their inquiries, threaten to cut off their inheritance, make an example out of the most aggressive one to set the tone for others. Force them to follow your lead.

CHAPTER THREE

IS THE TIMING RIGHT?

GOOD BASEBALL PLAYERS WON'T ATTEMPT to steal home during the early innings of a game; the risk of getting caught is too high, especially compared to the safer probability of scoring in a more conventional way. You must also pick the right time to scam your mark. Starting too early could expose you as a con, lead to disinheritance, and alert your mark to protect against subsequent attempts. On the other hand, waiting too long could prevent you from ever going forward, especially if your mark's decreasing mental capacity leads to a springing power of attorney, or even worse, a court supervised conservatorship.

Time your scam to minimize risk and maximize take. Do so by comparing your personal needs to your anticipated inheritance and distribution date. Attempting a scam may be unwise if you stand to inherit an adequate sum in the near future by merely waiting for nature to take its course. . If you move now and get caught, you will probably become disinherited and lose it all. Of course, if you need the money now, waiting even a short period of time may not be an option.

Relationship Factors

The nature of your relationship with a mark could affect the timing of your strike. Here are some common relationship types and timing factors for your consideration:

Fiduciaries and Professionals. These include accountants, bankers, financial planners, trustees, conservators, business partners, lawyers, tax preparers, successor trustees, executors, administrators, personal representatives, agents acting under a power of attorney, and investment advisors. Those of you in this category should answer the following questions before going forward:

- Do you have the present authority and ability to transfer funds?
- Can you transfer funds without drawing unwanted attention?
- Did anyone see you sign a document acknowledging your fiduciary duties?
- Do you have the right to borrow money from your mark's trust?
- Will the transfer of funds create any recognizable tax consequences?
- Do you control all financial decision-making responsibilities?
- Can you justify a reduction in the value of your mark's assets?
- Can you afford a skilled forensic accountant if needed?

Caregivers. Caregivers provide assistance to those who are no longer capable of taking care of their normal day-to-day needs. Their duties include everything from housekeeping, bathing, grooming, cooking, shopping, and running errands. Caregivers can be trained professionals, family members, or friends. Those of you in this category should answer the following questions before going forward:

- Does your mark have valuables inside the house?
- Is your mark isolated from family and friends?
- Is your mark susceptible to your influence?
- Is your mark aware of her assets?
- Are you being watched?
- Are you providing extra uncompensated services (such as washing windows)?
- Do you enjoy a close relationship with your mark?

Religious Leaders. This includes ministers, pastors, priests, clergy, monks, nuns, deacons, masters, elders, rabbis, spiritual teachers and advisors, religious activists, bishops, imams, clerics, supreme masters, cardinals, chaplains, theologians, and religious leadership councils. In short, it includes anyone who holds influence over another due to religious beliefs, teachings, and associations. Those of you in this category should answer the following questions before going forward:

- Is your mark a committed believer?
- Is your mark loyal to you personally?
- Does your mark regularly contribute to your religious organization?
- Does your mark have adequate disposable income?
- Is your mark bonded with immediate family members?

Blended Families. When parents get divorced and at least one remarries, a blended family is created. If your biological parent is your mark, then you will likely battle with a step-parent or a step-sibling. If your mark is involved with a blended family, answer the following questions before going forward:

- Is your mark infirm, dependent, or incapacitated?
- Is the relationship between you and your step-parent or step-sibling dependent on the one between you and your mark? (In other words, would the relationship continue after your biological parent's death?)
- Does your mark currently favor the step-parent or step-sibling?
- Can you have private communications with your mark?
- Do you provide most of your mark's care?
- Does the step-parent have biological children?

Adult Children. If your mark is a parent, answer the following questions before going forward:

- Do you have a strong bond?
- Is your mark more likely to seek help from you before anyone else?
- Does your mark view you as loyal, trustworthy and reliable?

All Others. For everyone else, answer the following questions before going forward:

- Are you well liked and respected by your mark?

- Does your mark owe you a favor?
- Have you demonstrated a history of loyalty?
- Do those in your mark's social circle hold you in high esteem?
- Do you have the ability to influence your mark's financial decisions?
- Does your mark depend on you for anything?
- Does your mark seem happy to see you during visits?

The nature of your relationship plays a vital role in timing your move. The relationship factors should help you evaluate the quality of your association. Your answers will provide all of the background information necessary for completing your timing analysis. You have to look at the bigger picture.

Now it's time to evaluate your mark's mental capacity to determine his level of vulnerability to scams. This is called the three stages of inheritance theft vulnerability.

* * *

Stages of Vulnerability

There are three stages of inheritance theft vulnerability: Stage One begins when your mark starts experiencing the mental challenges of advanced aging. He is still competent but is starting to complain about short term memory loss. He might regularly comment about having "senior moments." Stage Two begins when your mark's mental capacity is so weakened he can't manage his daily activities. During this stage, your mark clearly has long-term memory loss. Stage Three begins when your mark dies. Recognizing your mark's level of vulnerability is essential in planning your move. Using a Stage One approach on a Stage Two mark would lead to complete failure. So be careful. Let's go over each stage in more detail.

STAGE ONE: During Your Mark's Advancing Years

Seniors represent 12% of the U.S. population, but make up 35% of all fraud victims—and that's just the reported cases. They are the most vulnerable group in our population. That vulnerability can be attributed to several factors:

- They have assets;
- They are charitable;
- They come from a more trusting generation, which creates an opportunity for abuse;
- They are lonely and willing to talk to strangers;
- They are at home alone while other family members are working, making them easy prey, and
- Their diminishing mental capacity increases their level of susceptibility to scams.

You can identify a Stage One mark because they are usually retired seniors. They tend to have moments of confusion concerning their medical condition, current events and personal finances. They struggle with recalling information. Some occasionally neglect their personal hygiene. They stop bathing, brushing their teeth, shaving and combing their hair. When confronted, they playfully dismiss concerns by saying something like, "I am too old to worry about looking for a date."

It is best to strike Stage One marks that also suffer from disabling conditions such as dementia, bipolar disorder, or alcoholism. When combined with advancing age, marks with disabilities have severe cognitive impairments. The following is an example of a pair of cons taking advantage of a typical Stage One mark with mild cognitive impairment:

(The telephone rings)

Mark (Answers): "Hello?"

Con (Young girl): "Hi Grandpa. My car broke down in the desert; can you send $550 dollars? Please don't tell mom. She doesn't know I am out here."

Mark (Doesn't recognize caller, but is afraid to ask her name): "Speak up, I can't hear very well. Where are you?"

Con: "I am near Palm Springs. It's about 115 degrees out here, and we don't have enough money to pay the guy to fix our radiator. Can you send him $550 for me—here he is now. (She hands the phone to her partner, 'the mechanic.')

Con's Partner (Mechanic): "I don't have a lot of time. She told me that you would help. Can I have your credit card number or not?"

Mark: "I guess it is okay. Let me get it for you."

The mark didn't confirm the girl's name because he was unsure of his own mental capacity. Asking for a grandchild's name (he should already know) could reveal a weakness he would rather keep hidden. Your mark may fear losing his independence if anyone discovers his deteriorating mental capacity. Use that to your advantage.

Grandparents treasure their grandchildren, and as the telephone call illustrates, they are often willing to take chances when a grandchild's perceived safety is at stake. A grandparent-grandchild relationship creates additional susceptibility for Stage One marks. A grandchild has an advantage over most cons targeting Stage One marks. She is the subject of unconditional love.

Stage One marks have difficulty deflecting the advances of skilled cons. They can't resist the persistence of a charming caller pulling a scam. One famous scam involves a caller who congratulates the mark on winning a sweepstakes—one he never entered—and offering cash and prizes if he sends a check to cover the "required" federal income tax withholding. The con cashes the check and moves to the next mark.

I recently received an e-mail from a potential client wanting to know if he could use a power of attorney to help his 85-year-old widowed grandmother file for bankruptcy. He said she had substantial credit card debt and had depleted the home equity loan on her house. This call caught my attention because he failed to mention anything about his grandmother having medical expenses. Why would an 85 year-old widow run-up credit card debt? Why would she cash out the equity in her home?

Seniors on fixed incomes are fiscally conservative. They follow carefully planned budgets. I suspect the caller drove his grandmother into bankruptcy by depleting her assets and credit. He was pushing bankruptcy to wipe out any creditor's claims against his grandmother's estate before she dies. Doing so would maximize the value of her estate, as some assets are protected from creditors in bankruptcy proceedings. It appears that he committed fraud against the creditors to gain instant access to funds that won't have to be repaid due to the bankruptcy. That scam was well played.

The desire to help others, the dread of loneliness, their trusting nature, the fear of losing independence, and the relenting aging process make Stage One marks susceptible to scams. Many of them are exposed to risks before their mental awareness is ever called into question. Your success or failure will turn on the ability to recognize and seize these opportunities. If you spot one, act swiftly because the window could close when your mark enters Stage Two.

STAGE TWO: When Your Mark Loses Capacity

Stage Two begins when your mark's mental awareness becomes so weakened she can no longer take care of herself. She has noticeably decreasing brain function. The transition from Stage One to Stage Two doesn't occur suddenly. It happens gradually and silently. She may have good days and bad days. She may be lucid in the morning and incoherent in the afternoon. It is best to act during the transition person between these two stages because your mark's level of unprotected susceptibility his at its peak. Your mark is not only susceptible to coercion, undue influence, duress, fraud, and mistakes, but she lacks the ability to protect herself from your persuasion.

In Stage Two, you must act before your mark's decision making authority is replaced by a fiduciary, such as an agent under a power of attorney or a conservator (unless you are the agent or conservator). Most seniors reach a point where it's obvious they can no longer live independently. If your mark executed a power of attorney before losing capacity, the power of attorney will likely spring into effect once her doctor determines that she can no longer provide self-care. When that happens, her agent under the power of attorney will take control over her daily decisions, including the management of her financial assets. If your mark doesn't have a power of attorney, then someone will file a petition with the probate court seeking an appointment as her conservator. In either event, your opportunity substantially decreases once fiduciaries get involved.

STAGE THREE: When Your Mark Dies

Inheritance theft vulnerability isn't limited to various phases of your mark's life. Stage Three begins when your mark passes away. Unlike the first two stages, Stage Three is immediately recognizable. It's a terrific time to raid your mark's house, destroy his estate plan, and forge his name on a new estate plan. It's also the period when your duties as successor trustee can be used as a front for satisfying personal desires. When possible, start executing Stage Three scams while beneficiaries are mourning the loss of your mark. The length of mourning is different for each beneficiary. It can last from a couple of weeks to several months. It's hard to predict, and usually depends on a combination of how suddenly your mark died, and the nature and extent of his relationship to the mourner. A strong bond, coupled with a sudden and unexpected death, usually results in a longer grieving period. Once the grieving process is over, each beneficiary will shift their attention to getting their inheritance. So plan accordingly. The longer you wait to start your scam, the harder it is to finish because beneficiaries will stop grieving and start asking questions.

Raiding your mark's house requires some discipline. Only take items with significant monetary value. All other items, especially those with sentimental value should be collected, accounted for and stored for future distribution. Fight emotional impulses to lift family heirlooms. Stealing grandma's handmade quilt is sure to cause a stir with the beneficiaries. Besides, liquid assets should be your primary goal. Go for stockpiles of gold, silver, and cash; they are difficult to trace. Consider skimming from coin and stamp collections, and taking valuable pieces of art. Skip the jewelry (especially if it's been promised to someone else), photographs, the family Bible, video tapes, and awards. On the other hand, if you hold a fiduciary position as the successor trustee of your mark's trust or the executor of his estate, then accurately accounting of household items could make beneficiaries drop their guard, which could help you take more lucrative assets like real estate and brokerage accounts.

Cons in fiduciary positions, such as successor trustees and executors, have a distinct advantage over beneficiaries. If you are a successor trustee, you have the duty to administer the trust. In so doing, you have broad discretion over the identification, collection, valuation, distribution, and disbursement of assets. You can steal some assets without any real threat of detection. As an executor, you have additional advantages, but because the probate process is open, organized, and supervised by a probate judge, it is more difficult to convert traceable assets to yourself without drawing attention. Pay more attention to untraceable assets such as precious metals, jewelry and cash, and properly account for traceable assets like brokerage accounts and certificates of deposits. Remember, beneficiaries have the right to receive periodic accountings of trust assets, debts, income, and expenses. They can verify your reports by reviewing supporting documents such as bank statements.

Stage Three is also an excellent time to change your mark's estate plan. There are three acceptable ways. First, you can destroy all wills and trusts. Without them, your mark's estate will transfer to her heirs according to the rules of intestate succession. Intestate succession is a comprehensive process, but if an unmarried mark dies leaving three children, her estate will be divided equally between each child. If she has only one child, he will receive everything. Before destroying any documents, make sure you benefit more from intestate succession than your mark's current estate plan. You can do so by researching intestate succession laws.

Second, you can create a new will or trust in your mark's name. It should revoke prior wills and trusts and give you all or some of your mark's estate. Simply forge her name to make it valid. Third, you can amend your mark's will or trust, by adding yourself as a beneficiary, increasing your beneficiary share, or both. It will also require your mark's forged signature. You must match signing dates on all instruments to times your mark was most lucid. Take possession of the original estate plan before deciding to make any changes. If copies were made, gather them too. Once you have the originals and copies, read them carefully for the purpose of determining your beneficiary interest.

∗ ∗ ∗

When It's Too Late to Act

It's too late to act when the risks of exposure outweigh the benefits of success. Your risk of getting caught increases as your mark becomes hardened through awareness of their vulnerability to inheritance theft. Some marks take precautions once they become aware of their exposure. The following are signs that your mark is being protected:

- Your mark is "conserved," that is, he is protected by a conservator, someone appointed to make decisions on his behalf (unless you are the conservator);
- Your mark is no longer the trustee of his trust (unless you are the successor trustee);
- Your mark is no longer isolated;
- You're confronted about suspicious behavior regarding your mark's assets and you have not prepared an adequate explanation;
- Estate planning documents have been moved to a more secure location;
- People within your mark's social circle are asking questions about his assets;
- A family meeting is called to discuss your mark's failing mental capacity (unless you are a family member); or Family members are making an effort to protect your mark's assets.

If any of these signs are present, you should consider finding a softer mark. Going forward at this point is a mistake because the chances of getting caught are high. Good cons know when to seize an opportunity and when to let it go. In this game, you can always deal yourself a new hand by picking a new mark.

* * *

Case Notes

BROTHERLY LOVE

PETER WAS A 47-YEAR-OLD terminally ill man with a few

months to live. He called my firm asking for help because his brother was trying to throw him out of a house he shared with his recently deceased mother. He was too weak to meet at the office so I made a house call. Upon arrival, I had an uneasy feeling because his place looked run-down and abandoned. The fenced yard was covered with overgrown weeds and bushes. The front gate was hanging sideways, held up by the bottom hinge. It was too quiet, too still, and covered in too much dust. It was lifeless.

As I approached the rusted front screen door, I heard a man's worn voice say, "Come on in, it's open." Apparently he saw me pull up. The house was so dark I couldn't see anything, but the voice directed me to the kitchen table. While walking, I noticed a dark shadow of a man approaching my flank. The area was slightly illuminated by a single candle in the middle of the table. I hurried to the light and waited as the man approached in slow, unsteady steps. He sat across from me. The candle's glow revealed a prematurely aged face with pale skin, yellow sunken eyes, and a mustache with long sideburns that were more fashionable a hundred and fifty years ago than today. While searching my briefcase for a pen and notepad, the man stated, "My brother stole my Navy-issued cap and ball Colt revolver." I suddenly felt an uneasy chill, as though I was in the presence of a Civil War ghost.

Peter wasn't a ghost. He was a terminally ill man whose impending death was hastened by the despicable acts of his brother Richard. Peter was a man of little means. When he got sick, his mother insisted that he move in with her. Several months later, his mother unexpectedly died. She left a fully-funded trust for Peter and Richard's benefit. Richard was the trustee of that trust. He was also a successful banker who lived in Japan. Upon hearing the news of his mother's death, Richard returned to California for a month. He ransacked his mother's house and tried using his authority as trustee to force Peter out.

Peter was defenseless. He had no money, no place to go, and was preparing for his own demise. Rather than make Peter comfortable, which was within his discretion as trustee of the Trust, Richard was forcing Peter out of the house. Richard shut off the utilities. He had them specially locked so they could not be turned on without his permission. Within two weeks, Peter was without water, electricity and food. Richard was supposed to distribute his mother's assets between himself and Peter in equal shares. Plus he had the authority to make preliminary distributions because his mother left $80,000 cash in her savings account. But Richard refused to give Peter any money. He was waiting for Peter to die so he could take it all for himself.

According to trust terms, if one brother dies before receiving his full share of the assets, the remaining balance would go to the surviving brother. Richard was trying to take full advantage of that clause. By putting his own interests above Peter's, however, Richard was also breaching his trustee duties. That was all we needed to seek his removal as trustee.

Within ten days, we replaced Richard with a neutral trustee. The neutral was ordered to make a preliminary distribution to Peter. The payment wasn't much, but it was enough to turn on the utilities, buy food and medication, and make Peter comfortable. He died six weeks later surrounded by strangers.

STEP 2

ARE THE RIGHT PLAYERS IN PLACE?

"I always thought that record would stand until it was broken." ~ *Yogi Berra*

BASE RUNNERS WON'T ATTEMPT TO steal home unless there is a left-handed pitcher on the mound and the batter is struggling. It's simply too difficult steal against right-handed pitchers because they have a natural view of the base runner during their windup. It defies common sense to attempt to steal a base when the batter has a reasonable chance of getting him home with a base hit, especially when the pitcher is staring him down. The same principles apply here. You should only attempt to make a move when the right people are in place. Who are the right people? You will know after targeting your mark.

CHAPTER FOUR

TARGETING YOUR MARK

SAVVY CONS DON'T RANDOMLY PULL names out of a hat when picking marks. They go through a careful selection process called targeting. Targeting involves the identification of potential marks, the collection of their personal information and an evaluation of their vulnerabilities. They recognize the difference between hard and soft marks. Hard marks are well insulated against scams. They sometimes have multiple layers of protection. Soft marks are utterly defenseless. Most marks fall between those two extremes. Aim for the softest one possible.

Finding soft marks for a one-time scam is a matter of targeting someone within your family unit, social circles, or business associations. He could be an aging parent, friend, or business partner. He could be a stage two dependent relative that gave you power of attorney over their assets or a probate or trust estate left by a recently deceased unattached friend. . In those cases, targeting is not difficult because the mark will fall into your lap.

Perpetual cons work a little harder because they tend to target marks outside their immediate family, social and business circles. Certified public accountants, bankers, clergymen, doctors, lawyers, mental health professionals, financial planners, tax preparers, political leadesr, or someone actively involved in social organizations have specific advantages. Such associations will bring you into contact with many marks, just look around the office. If that's still too close some cons are disguised as perfect strangers, helpful neighbors, polite sales associates, domestic service providers or concerned social advocates. Do you work with infirm seniors? Are you a professional caregiver, private professional fiduciary, conservator, or trustee? Are you the head of a fictitious charitable organization pretending to provide a public service? If so, you are in the best position to target a soft mark. Take aim.

Targeting

When you think of a mark, you naturally think of infirm benefactors. Although they make satisfactory marks, and are the focus in this chapter, don't narrow the pool of your potential marks to people. Trusts and estates make excellent marks. Consider targeting, what many consider the best marks, a revocable or irrevocable trust, probate estate, conservatorship estate, or any other entity managed by someone with fiduciary responsibilities. Those entities, however, are usually targeted by cons with present management power and authority, such as, conservators, agents, trustees, personal representatives, executors, and administrators.

Gaining Trust

When targeting potential marks, favor those that either view you as trustworthy or with whom you can build a trusting relationship. If you need to build trust, do it through regular interaction. In my experience, seniors are more trusting than their children. They don't have time to build new relationships using conventional methods. Determine whether your potential mark is capable of trusting anyone. Does she have the mental capacity to understand a trusting relationship? Do you have the ability to discreetly contact her on a regular basis? If so, can you communicate with her in person or over the telephone? You can you write letters, but it takes longer and is inherently more risky, as others might read the letters and get wise to your intentions. Here are five tips for building trust:

Do what you say. Your word must be golden. Always follow through. If you say you're going to call your mark on Tuesday at 10:00 a.m., do it. Savvy cons even create opportunities to build trust by intentionally making and keeping a series of small promises, such as calling to discuss television soap operas.

Never get caught lying. Instead, seek opportunities to tell the truth, even if doing so hurts a little. If you never get caught in a lie, you'll be appreciated for your honesty. Honesty is a character trait highly valued by benefactors, and voluntarily sharing an embarrassing truth conveys honesty.

Give details. Even when you have a chance to make general comments don't do it. Instead, give clear, detailed accounts. If asked where you went to college, don't say "in Oregon." Say, "Oregon State University. I got a degree in biology." Details indicate you have nothing to hide. Omitting even minor details could raise suspicion, so communicate with specificity.

Don't exaggerate. Although it might seem okay to overstate a point, doing so is risky. If asked what you did with your biology degree, don't say "I went into biotech and worked on vaccine research," unless it's true. Better to say "I took a shot at the biotech industry, but it turned out I couldn't make a living as a scientist." If your mark perceives puffing as a lie, an exaggerated fact will erode trust.

Always keep secrets. Don't gossip or tell your mark secrets you have with others. Although it might temporarily capture her interest, it will also send the message that you can't be trusted.

The nature of your relationships and your ability to build trust should be considered when targeting a mark. Those two factors will help narrow the field and lead you in the right direction. There is more to consider, so let's move on.

After targeting a potential mark, collect his personal information. Learn his age, level of independence, medical condition, social activities, family relationships, involvement in situational control, and his ability to defend against scams. If your mark is a trust or estate, this information is less valuable, but you should collect it on the trustee.

Age

The age factor merits a discussion because advancing age is related to memory loss and benefactors suffering from memory loss make good marks. Studies show that people start losing brain cells in their twenties. As brain cells decrease, so does their ability to recall recent memory. Although knowing one's age is essential in starting your analysis, it is somewhat meaningless without additional information.

Memory loss isn't triggered by a specific age. Its onset occurs gradually and sometimes much later in life. Some people in their 90s have the minds of a steel trap. As of this writing, United States District Court Judge Wesley E. Brown is still hearing cases at 103 years of age. And he's still not the oldest practicing federal judge in the history of the United States. Learning more about memory function will help you better understand your mark's mental capacity independent of age.

There are three types of memory functions you need to know: One, temporary short term memory; Two, long term recent memory; and Three, long term remote memory.

Temporary short term memory is the type used to remember a plumber's phone number you retrieved from a phone book long enough to dial the telephone. Long term recent memory is the type used for recalling what you had for lunch. And long term remote memory is the type that helps you recall certain events experienced during your childhood.

Older marks tend to have more difficulty with their recent memory. Recent memory is necessary for carrying out complex cognitive tasks such as learning, reasoning, and comprehending new information. Recognizing the differences in these types of memory functions will help you identify marks battling with their memory issues. Zero in on those who often forget things associated with recent memory, such as the names of people they just met, places they visited on a tour, or what they had for breakfast.

Recent memory can be evaluated by conducting a memory span test, which establishes the number of items (usually words) a subject can immediately retain and recall. In a typical memory span test, the examiner reads a list of 10 words, at the rate of one a second. The test taker is then asked to recite the list in order. The average recall for normal functioning adults is seven items. Obviously giving a formal memory span test to a potential mark is not smart, but it doesn't hurt to evaluate him in a more passive manner.

Marks will experience some recent memory loss if their advancing age is coupled with high levels of stress. That stress may be caused by the loss of a spouse, or any of the following medical conditions: alcoholism, Alzheimer's disease, dementia, depression, drug abuse, encephalitis, meningitis, brain tumor, HIV/AIDS, Parkinson's disease, seizure (epilepsy), stroke, head trauma, malnutrition, neurodegenerative disease, psychological or emotional disorders, prolonged toxin exposure, sleep disorders, thyroid disease, or vitamin deficiencies.

Infirm marks suffering from moderate to severe medical conditions are probably experiencing recent memory loss, but you should also look for one or more of the following signs:

- Memory changes that disrupt daily life.
- Challenges in planning or solving problems.
- Difficulty completing familiar tasks at home.
- Confusion with time or place.
- Trouble understanding visual or spatial relationships.
- New problems with words in speaking or writing.
- Misplacing things and losing the ability to retrace steps.
- Decreased or poor judgment.
- Withdrawal from work or social activities.
- Changes in mood or personality.

Marks suffering from (severe) recent memory loss often do not recognize their symptoms. This is fantastic news because they are highly susceptible to undue influence, coercion, fraud, and menace. They are easily manipulated. Is the targeting process starting to make sense? Keep reading because there's a lot more to learn.

Medical Status

Pay close attention to a target's medical condition. Infirm targets are defenseless and highly susceptible to scams.. Medical records are confidential, so it may be difficult for outsiders to get specific information about a target's health. You will have to rely on personal observations and perhaps information from unsuspecting third parties. For insiders, learning about a target's medical status is simple. Ask them how they feel. Review medical bills. You can learn all about their medication by reading prescription bottles in their medicine cabinet. Take your target to her doctor's appointments. It's actually quite easy because most infirm benefactors need rides to their doctors and are usually willing to discuss their medical condition with any caring person willing to listen. Be comforting and supportive; show you care.

Level of Independence

Seniors typically value their independence. Yet many gradually become dependent on others without the benefit of a conservatorship or power of attorney. Dependency is caused by the natural deterioration of physical and mental capacities. The need for care usually falls on family members, especially middle-aged children and their spouses. The level of dependence is different for each benefactor, but progressively worsens with time. Some need help with transportation, some with check writing, and some need assistance bathing and grooming. Your chances of pulling a scam improve as your target becomes more dependent on others—especially if he is dependent on you.

Social Activities

Social activities include visits from friends, attending social events, or participation in organized activities. Some targets are naturally more social than others. For purposes of targeting, favor people with recently changed social patterns. If a target played Bingo every Friday night, but for no apparent reason stops going, take aim. She is a good candidate. Targets that withdraw from social activities typically lose contact with their network of friends and become isolated. Isolation is a tool you should use when possible. If you have enough influence, encourage your isolated target to stay away from friends. Create rumors. Accuse them of plotting to steal your target's money, trying to declare her incompetent, or forcing her into a nursing home.

Family Relationships

Families give benefactors a sense of identity by providing them with moral, social and economic support. They also protect them from cons. Yet it seems that some families don't understand the importance of keeping benefactors close. Take advantage of those families by targeting benefactors living alone. They are more willing to discuss financial matters with strangers and establish new relationships, particularly with regular visitors. It is much easier to bond with isolated benefactors than those surrounded by family. If you're polite, isolated benefactors will agree to just about anything to keep you from leaving them alone. There is an added bonus: Poor family relationships substantially reduce your risk of detection.

Situational Control

Who has control over your target's socialization, privacy, and care? Knowing this will help you evaluate her level of vulnerability. With any luck, it will be the target herself, especially if she's infirm. Infirm targets are susceptible to all sorts of scams. But they also tend to have "minders." It could be her husband, sibling, or friend. It could also be a professional care provider, agent, or perhaps a doctor. Find out who's in control and turn your attention to evaluating that person's level of involvement in your target's affairs. Minders represent stability and security. They help targets function independently. Minders are energetic, balanced, confident, and well organized. He may also have above average intelligence and a clear understanding of your target's social, financial, and medical situation. In other words, that person is a bodyguard. The more he's involved with the details of your target's life, the less likely your scam will work.

Information Accessibility

Target people that fail to protect their personal information, financial records, and estate plans.. It doesn't get much better than unfettered access to an infirm mark's full name, date of birth, place of birth, social security number, driver's license, passport, usernames and passords.. Try to get original copies of anything containing your mark's signature including social security cards, driver's license, and handwritten letters and cards. These items can be extremely useful if you decide to forge her signature on wills, trusts, power of attorney forms, deeds, payment on death designations and other asset transfer instruments. Plus, having original documents in your possession will prevent others from giving them to handwriting experts to challenge instruments you forge.

Having access to your mark's financial information will open many doors. You can get the names and locations of financial institutions, ascertain account numbers, and identify deposits and expenses. You can use it to designate new account beneficiaries, write checks, set up automatic deposits of investment income or social security checks into your personal account, or to become a joint holder on the accounts. Retaining original financial documents could also prevent your mark, and others, from discovering your activities until it's too late.

Targeting a mark for an inheritance theft scam is not that difficult, especially when the benefactor is infirm. Just ask yourself a few questions. Is she susceptible to my influence? Is she incapable of protecting herself? And, is she isolated and lonely? Did she fail to protect her personal information, financial documents, usernames and passwords, and estate plans? Does she trust you? And did she give you situational control? The likelihood of success increased each time you answered yes..

* * *

Case Notes

THE WILY WEALTH MANAGER

AFTER 52 YEARS OF SELF-MANAGING their investments, Robert and Laura Arlington set out to hire a wealth manager. They grew their portfolio to nearly $400,000 by buying and holding dividend producing stocks from their employer, Southern California Edison. Robert is now looking forward to his golden years in retirement.

Conrad Smith prepared income tax returns for the Arlington's over past several years. Since he had served them well and knew just about everyone in town, Robert contacted him for a referral. Conrad is known for helping people get just about anything, from a gourmet duck soup recipe to a deck of marked playing cards. Conrad made it his business to be the go-to guy in town. It was part of his successful marketing strategy.

Conrad received Robert's call with the pleasantries of a seasoned salesman. Within 30 seconds he offered his "wealth management services." His voice roared with enthusiasm as he explained all the benefits of using him to prepare taxes and manage their retirement accounts. The Arlington's had always like Conrad; most people did. His charm and social grace is unmatched in the community. His smile is always followed by quick-witted comments, which make him fun to be around. Their decision to hire was easy, albeit based more on their emotions than his qualifications.

Over the years Conrad's relationship with the Arlington's grew into a friendship. He saw them numerous times at social functions, and met regularly to prepare tax returns and to discuss investment strategies. Within seven years, Conrad prepared their estate plan and became the trustee of their living trust. He also became their agent under a power of attorney for both asset management and medical care. Conrad's relationship grew as he was charged with all the duties and obligations of a professional fiduciary. The Arlington's loved him like a son. Childless and estranged from family, the Arlington's decided to pass their wealth to Conrad. He was an agreeable person with exceptional interpersonal warmth and sensitivity. Choosing him as their beneficiary seemed rational to them, and the casual observer.

Shortly after his 77th birthday, Robert suffered a heart attack and died. Conrad was there comforting Laura and assisting her with the arrangements. He knew the local funeral director and pastor. He was clearly an enormous help to Laura. He also mourned Robert's passing. The two had grown close over the years. Some would say their bond was more like father and son than friends. During the memorial, Conrad eulogized Robert. He made the customary comments about how Robert was adored by his friends and co-workers, and recounted stories of devotion to his wife Laura. He ended by saying that Robert was the only real father he ever knew.

Robert's death was especially hard on Laura. The home they built together was suddenly empty. As the protected homemaker, she was entirely dependent on Robert. She needed someone trustworthy for support. She had no idea how to fill the void left by Robert's passing. She didn't know how to pay the utility bills, service the cars, or maintain the house. Once again, Conrad was there. Laura was in such need, she asked him to assume full responsibility over all financial matters—which he did.

Conrad was comfortable with his new role at the Arlington home. He paid the bills on time each month and kept the house and car in excellent repair. Of course, Laura offered to pay Conrad, but he waived off any talk of compensation. He knew someday he would inherit the entire estate. He enjoyed keeping Laura comfortable—plus staying close helped him protect his inheritance.

Years before Robert's death he did something that would ultimately change the course of his legacy. At Conrad's direction, he opened and transferred all of his funds to an online stock brokerage account. He then gave Conrad the username and password. Conrad said doing so would save money because online trading fees were a lot less than the commissions charged by his full service brokerage. But, Conrad failed to mention the risks of allowing unrestricted access to the account or his lack of credentials to trade online using Robert's name or that using his firm's research to buy and sell stocks was theft. Conrad had the spirit of a caring friend and the mind of a shrewd opportunist.

After Robert's death, Laura needed more attention than Conrad had imagined. She called daily with honey-do lists. Laura was lonely, and Conrad knew the lists were her way of generating contact. Once again, Laura instructed Conrad to pay himself for the work. This time he accepted the offer. To access funds, he set up another account using Laura's online broker. In violation of his duties under the power of attorney, he started transferring money from the Laura's account into his own. He then used the money in both accounts to engage in risky futures and options trading. A legitimate wealth manager would never do such a thing under the circumstances.

Conrad started by transferring a few thousand dollars at a time, and eventually took larger chunks of twenty to fifty thousand. After six months, he had taken about half of Laura's life savings. Surprisingly, he earned an impressive 20% return on his trades.

As Laura grew infirm, she had no way of monitoring Conrad's activities. She didn't appear harmed because she drew enough income from retirement and Social Security to support her modest standard of living. Conrad felt justified because he was going to inherit it all when Laura died. Apparently he forgot about his duties and obligations as a fiduciary, and that Laura had the right to disinherit him at any time.

Nine months later the online broker's fraud department noticed the transfers. They didn't know the background facts, nor did they seem to care. By then Conrad had transferred nearly all of Laura's money into his personal account. The fraud department determined that Laura may have been the victim of fraudulent activity, so they reported their findings to the County's Public Guardian. Within one week, the Public Guardian obtained an order temporarily removing Conrad as the agent under Laura's power of attorney and as successor trustee of the Arlington Family Trust. The County knew they had a strong case against Conrad because they had brokerage statements reflecting the transfers. They threatened to seek damages totaling three times the money he took. The Deputy Public Guardian called Conrad several times, threatening to take his house and freeze his bank accounts unless he fully cooperated.

Laura became mentally incapacitated after suffering a serious stroke. A conservator was appointed to look after her financial and personal needs. Laura was not capable of expressing why Conrad's actions should go unpunished. All Conrad could do was point out that some of the transferred funds were compensation for past services. He also argued that his (fraudulent) behavior should be excused because Laura wasn't harmed, and he was the sole beneficiary. The Public Guardian didn't buy any of those excuses. In taking more than $400,000, Conrad committed multiple breaches of his fiduciary duties. The County wanted to make an example out of him; mostly because they had a strong case. In an effort to save his home, Conrad agreed to settle by returning the misappropriated funds and waiving 50% of his inheritance under the trust. Laura's next of kin inherited the remaining trust assets.

STEP 3

IS THE PITCHER WINDING UP?

"We made too many wrong mistakes." ~ *Yogi Berra*

PITCHERS ARE SO SUCCESSFUL HOLDING runners on third base, they are starting to abandon the set position and pitch from a full windup. That's what they did before the set became popular in the 1950s. Is stealing home now so obsolete that it's viable?

Always look for opportunities created out of complacency. Target people that are so sure nothing will happen they fail to protect their assets from scams. Better yet, zero in on those who are so pleased with their efforts to protect assets, they don't think inheritance theft is possible.

CHAPTER FIVE

ATTACK COMPLACENCY

COMPLACENCY IS GENERALLY DEFINED AS "unjustified self-satisfaction accompanied by a low awareness of the need for action or involvement." A psychologist might define it as, "A conscious or unconscious relaxation of one's usual standards in making decisions and taking action." A coal miner was once asked "What is the difference between ignorance and complacency?" He responded by saying, "I don't know and I don't care."

People gloss over bank statements containing numerous entries because analyzing data rich documents strains the subconscious and emotional mind. That kind of overload creates complacency. People see all those numerical entries and shut down. They don't want to commit to the tedious task of reconciling each transaction. Diligent is achieve through a conscious mind. It requires work, but that's the only way to detect fraudulent entries.

Regardless of how it's defined or why it occurs, complacent seniors create opportunity for easy scams. Target those that are easy-going in how they receive information, who they receive it from, how they secure valuables, how they safeguard important documents, how they protect their sources of income; how they manage lines of credit, and about the company they keep.

Seniors That Fail to Screen Phone Calls

The telephone is a powerful tool for some scams. Complacent seniors answer telephone calls directly. They reject technology such as caller ID and answering machines to screen calls. Most don't understand how to use them and are not interested in learning. These seniors are easy to reach for telephone swindles and for building high levels of trust for lucrative scams.

Seniors That Fail to Register on "Do Not Call" Lists

The National "Do Not Call Registry" helps consumers block unwanted telemarketing calls at home. Seniors that fail to register their telephone numbers may be contacted for legitimate pitches. If you are pushing telephone swindle scams, then target retired seniors with unregistered numbers. Hopefully, you will find one suffering from diminished mental capacity. If so, sell her all kinds of things she doesn't need, and remember to supersize the order.

Seniors You Can Reach By Mail

Late Stage One or early Stage Two seniors with access to unmonitored mail are practically inviting you into their living rooms. They love to read letters. Creative writers can build strong relationships with these seniors through the mail. Handwritten letters appear more trustworthy and compelling so avoid using a word processor. Depending on your scam preference, you might want to engage them in frequent and continuous letter writing campaigns. Consider starting with a greeting card.

Seniors That Embrace Charitable Giving

Charitable organizations spend millions of dollars each year identifying and nurturing donors. Mailing lists of verified contributors are easy to obtain through the internet. Infirm seniors are especially desirable. Their willingness to help anyone promoting a noble cause, coupled with their complacency in researching the creditability of charitable organizations makes them particularly susceptible. You can scam them by creating fictitious organizations with charitable sounding purposes (Charity scams are discussed in Chapter 9). If you can touch the hearts of infirm seniors, you will easily pull increasing contributions each donation cycle.

Seniors Stockpiling Cash and Valuables

Some of the older seniors were affected by the great depression. They watched banks close doors on their parents. Nearly 50% of them lacked adequate food, shelter or medical care when they were young. Many suffered from rickets. Today, they still distrust banks. They hide large sums of cash, gold bullion, rare coins and other valuables around their homes. They have been doing it so long, some have no idea how much they have or where it is hidden. They have become complacent in securing their valuables. Cons with access to their homes could skim valuables without suspicion of wrongdoing.

Seniors with Open Lines of Credit

Seniors may use and pay off credit cards to maintain high credit ratings. Many have untapped home equity lines of credit for cash reserves in the event of emergencies. They may have held them for so long, they neither appreciate their associated risks, nor care to close them out. They represent creative opportunities for savvy cons. For example, it only takes one signed check to draw $50,000 against an equity line of credit. If your mark keeps a lot of credit cards, you can pull smaller scams using their cards without getting a signature. Not only are these types of scams easy to pull off, the transaction will probably go unnoticed for 30, 60 or 90 days, sometimes longer.

Seniors That Fail to Secure Important Documents

You probably know people who put unopened monthly statements in an "important papers" box. They might include quarterly brokerage statements, pension statements, and other financial documents. That same box may include an estate plan and tax returns. There are lots of seniors with those boxes. It might be in a filing cabinet, desk drawer, or hutch. It can be anywhere, but it is usually in a convenient and easily accessible location. Those boxes are rarely ever locked. Even when they are, they can be opened quite easily. The routine of storing important documents together in the usual place leads seniors into a false sense of security. Depending on the nature of your scam, you can capitalize on document complacency by taking the documents themselves or copying the information they contain. If you take the documents, you might want to make photocopies and replace the originals before anyone notices they are missing.

Seniors that Trust Too Readily

It is normal to trust deserving family members. This is especially true between spouses and between parents and their children. It's also normal to trust a close friend. When seniors base their trust on relationship type instead of relationship quality, they become susceptible to scams. This is called relationship complacency. It's where someone is given trust they didn't earn and don't deserve. That's good news because it means you can gain the trust of a late Stage One or early Stage Two senior based on your relationship type. It's not something you have to earn over time by proving your worthiness. It's handed to you because you are connected by family association or friendship.

Complacent marks also create opportunity for complacency scams. Complacency scams usually start on a small scale, such as "borrowing" money, but they can grow into something more substantial, like adding yourself on title to the mark's house. If played well, you can increase your take exponentially though a series of complacency scams.

* * *

Case Notes

THE GRABBING GRANDSON

HELEN IS ONE OF THE BEST conservators in Southern California. She treats conservatees with the unconditional kindness and respect of a loving grandmother. Her penny-accurate financial accountings are always supported with credible records. Courts routinely appoint her as a private professional fiduciary on complicated cases.

When she called with an "intriguing one," I knew it would be good. She said, "Ruth Fields is an 84-year-old woman with two close daughters and a grandson named Max. I was appointed as her conservator during an emergency hearing this morning because the bank is foreclosing on her home and she lacks the mental capacity to protect herself."

"Do you know how the house came into foreclosure?" I asked.

I could practically hear her smile as she said, "Bingo." Most 84-year-olds either don't have a mortgage or make timely mortgage payments. With close family members nearby, Ruth should have never fallen behind on hers. We both agreed that someone close to Ruth should have caught this earlier because incapacity doesn't occur overnight.

"Enough with that," Helen insisted. "It's time to work. About two years ago, Max coaxed Ruth into refinancing her house, to raise money, so he could "borrow" $100,000 for a mobile home. He contacted and provided the bank with Ruth's personal information and handled all communication between Ruth and the loan broker. Ruth wasn't even involved until it was time to sign documents. That's where this gets interesting. Why didn't anyone at the bank notice Ruth's absence? Why didn't anyone notice she was struggling at the time documents were signed?"

"Those are valid points, Helen, but lenders are not required to conduct capacity exams," I said.

"Of course not," she replied, "but they had to know that Ruth was being manipulated."

While explaining her case in more detail, Helen's voice slowly faded as the wheels in my head turned at full speed. Then it hit me. This is a contracts case! Helen's instincts are right. Even without a capacity examination the bank knew or should have known that Ruth lacked the capacity to enter into that mortgage. The bank didn't know about Ruth's waning capacity, but they cannot ignore the obvious. If they were reasonably attentive during the lending process, they would have known that Ruth didn't understand what was going on. If we prove they did the mortgage would be invalid.

"Hold on, Helen. I think you might have something here."

She said, "I knew you would think so."

"Helen, do you have any medical records regarding Ruth's capacity?"

"Yes. Her doctor diagnosed her with dementia six years ago. She was under his care at the time she signed those mortgage papers at the bank."

It was my turn to smile. Helen hired my firm to handle the elder abuse action and to stop foreclosure on Ruth's home. While reviewing documents subpoenaed from the bank, I learned that the broker who handled Ruth's second mortgage also worked on Max's mobile home loan. Acting as an agent for both of them was clearly a conflict of interest. We filed several petitions with the court against Max and the bank, alleging a variety of contract and elder abuse actions, including fraud and conspiracy to commit fraud. Within a matter of days, the foreclosure proceeding on Ruth's home was suspended. The bank then quickly settled by agreeing to invalidate the mortgage against Ruth and to pay all related fees and costs. They then sued Max to recover their damages and for payment on the mortgage.

STEP 4

GRADUALLY INCREASE YOUR LEAD

"You can observe a lot by watching." ~ Yogi Berra

GRADUALLY INCREASE YOUR LEAD OFF third base by taking a couple of small steps towards home plate. Go slow to avoid unnecessary attention, but move with a purpose. Once the pitcher sets his foot on the pitching mound rubber, start side-stepping down the line. Take three to four large strides. Stop once you get about 10 to 12 feet off third base and wait. Cons must also move steadily towards their objectives.

Now that you've targeted a senior, gather more information. Go out and do things together. Offer to take her for coffee or lunch. Position yourself to learn pertinent details about her life. She's no longer human; she's just a mark so fight the urge to bond. But during your time together, get her to open up and bond with you. Take control of the conversation by redirecting any questions she asks about your life back to her. If she asks about family origin answer in a friendly manner and in the same sentence redirect back to her with a specific question like, "We were originally from Seaford, Delaware. Where did you grow up?" Just keep following up with open-ended questions until she tells her life story. Once she gets rolling, the information will flow. Grease the wheels by acting interested through eye contact, head nodding and smiles. If you fail to acknowledge her comments, she will shut down.

If your mark is a stranger and nervous about meeting new people, make contact through one of her close friends. Create a situation where that person introduces the two of you. The friend's credibility will transfer to you and open the door to personal access.

Establish and nurture a close relationship with your new friend.. Look for opportunities to spend time together. Make thoughtful gestures to keep her spirits high. When appropriate, initiate longer more engaging conversations. Give her your full attention while she answers. Eliminate distractions; make sure she sees you shut off your cell phone. Almost everyone enjoys the sound of their name. So use hers frequently. Modulate your voice so its pitch and tone are pleasant to hear. Always wait until she's finished with a sentence before commenting; never interrupt her. When it's time to leave, end on an agreeable note and open the door for another visit. Say something like: "The childhood story about your pet pig Pinky was interesting, can you finish it over coffee some other time?"

If your mark is shielded by an inner circle of family and friends, getting close requires entry into the circle. Start by identifying the decision makers. In keeping with the baseball theme, let's call them the Owners. They have the power and duty to control the nature and future of the group. You must shake things up with the Owners. This is the only exception to the rule of avoiding attention. For example, point out a weakness in her home security system. Recommend a private security company capable of providing adequate services. By shaking things up with the Owners and offering solutions, you'll set yourself apart as a trustworthy and valuable resource. Those characteristics could give you inner circle status.

People are uncomfortable with change because it requires learning new things. Use that as your ticket. Put yourself in the position to be noticed by Owners and if given the opportunity, lead them through the change. Don't kick anyone out of their position, just create a new role—use your special talents—do something that will benefit the circle. Once you've assumed some power, cement your role. Do that by befriending other like-minded Owners. That part should be easy. Now that you are part of the inner circle, direct your focus to more productive tasks, like gaining your mark's trust.

CHAPTER SIX

THE SECRETS OF STEALTH

STEALTH IS THE ART OF moving covertly to avoid detection. Use it to minimize conflicts while planning and executing scams. Start by identifying your enemy. They are your mark's family members, friends, bankers, doctors, lawyers, accountants, business partners, conservators, trustees, personal representatives, and others within her circle. Your enemy is anyone standing between you and your inheritance theft goals. If you are surrounded, be wary but be glad: it means you are close to the goal. Their omnipresence makes the practice of stealth both necessary and challenging. Use the secrets of stealth to move around undetected.

Become Invisible

Becoming invisible starts with an understanding of how your true nature is detected by others. People make judgments about your though their eyes and ears. Fool their senses so their inferences are benign to your aims. Eyes see your movement first,, then they recognize silhouette and finally color. So the eyes see things in the following order: movement, silhouette and color. Next, when we hear a sound, our eyes tend to look for the cause at "eye level" because we have a natural tendency to look for the obvious. Very seldom do our eyes look up high or down low to seek the cause of noise.

My point is that people don't look too deeply into their surroundings. If what they see on the surface appears normal, they lack curiosity and the desire to investigate further.

Avoid Detection

To avoid detection, slow down your movement on all levels— especially the most observable. If someone is facing you (meaning if he is starting to suspect your bad intentions), stop moving. Put your observable actions on hold. Blend in with the natural elements in your environment by assuming your ostensible role and purpose within your surroundings. This will trick the eyes and the mind of your enemies. Your true intentions will go unnoticed, unless your actions are obviously contemptuous.

Conceal yourself in the darkest portion of shadows. Sneak, and hide your deeper strategies behind innocent actions. Crouch to appear small and insignificant. In other words, redirect attention to your surroundings, so you appear normal and routine. Avoid "light," as it can expose your true intentions. Remember that eyes see movement first. When faced with the risk of exposure, stop!

Unusual comments naturally arouse curiosity. But once assured it came from a reliable source, we cease investigation. Obviously it is best to avoid making noise, but if you must, then fool the ears. So what do I mean by noise? Noise is any comment that alert someone that inheritance theft is afoot. It includes, for example, comments about improper gifting, transfers of funds, title changes, financial positions, changing wills, amending trusts, and the creation of payment-on-death accounts. You can fool ears by suppressing noise.

Real World Application

Use natural sounds to mask noise. For example, if your scam involves amending a trust, then do so within the natural course of updating your mark's estate plan. Be careful to avoid words indicating any modification or changes "reflecting her current desires." They will ring loud enough to wake curiosity and compel investigation from people within her circle. .

Second, if your scam calls for a simple act, cover your true intentions with something plausible. For example, if your mark wants to update her brokerage account beneficiary designation to include her grandchildren, help her. Instead of writing her grandchildren's names on the actual bank card, write them down on a separate piece of paper and claim that it is an attachment. Ask her to sign the card, then write in your name as the 100% beneficiary.. Don't forget to discard the attachment before delivering the card. That simple act could make you the sole beneficiary of your mark's brokerage account.

Third, distract the enemy's sentry by introducing chaos. If you accidently draw unwanted curiosity during a scam, introduce a chaotic event to project unwanted attention in another direction. The enemy attribute your noise to that chaos. They will think it caused the noise and cease their investigation. For example, if you are caught shredding your mark's credit card statements to destroy evidence of cash advances taken for your personal benefit, create a diversion such as the receipt of a crime alert instructing people to destroy unnecessary documents to prevent identity theft.

Those are just a few examples of how to incorporate the art of stealth into your strategy. Using it takes some creativity. Become invisible by concealing your presence or creating diversions. Mastering this step alone can result in substantial gains.

CHAPTER SEVEN

AVOID ATTENTION

CAN YOU IMAGINE A CAT burglar wearing an orange reflective safety vest? Of course not; it defies common sense. Cat burglars use the cover of darkness as a tool to avoid detection. You should also avoid drawing attention to yourself. Unlike burglars, it is okay to let people see you; just don't give them any reason to dwell on your presence. In this chapter, you will learn how to become "invisible in plain sight."

Consider Your Surroundings

If your scam includes getting close to your mark during an event attended by others, ascertain the details of your surroundings in advance. Ask questions from those who have attended similar events in the past. At a minimum, review the guest list, dress code, and itinerary. Knowing these answers in advance will help you prepare for blending with the crowd.

Wear Common Clothing

It is always a good idea to copy the style and fashion of clothing worn by people around your mark. When it comes to attire, choose muted colors. Dress like an average Joe. Don't wear the tightest or baggiest clothes, the neatest or sloppiest hair style or attention grabbing shoes. In essence, don't wear anything that causes you to stand out.

Tone Down Conduct

Do what everyone else is doing, but to a lesser degree. If everyone is laughing, limit your expression to a soft chuckle; if the room is quiet, don't make any noise. Again, fit in without drawing unnecessary attention.

Minimize Eye Contact

Eyes are the windows of the soul. In other words, your subconscious thoughts are revealed through eye contact with others. This form of nonverbal communication exposes your feelings. Justifying your scam isn't enough to hide it from detection. It's still wrong, and it bothers you. Burying it through conscious justification helps on an emotional level, but it will not remove it from your soul—the subconscious. It remains there for everyone to see. Avoiding eye contact altogether will draw unwanted attention because it's the trait of a liar. When talking to the enemy, minimize eye contact by looking at their foreheads or by directing their attention to other reference points. Look at oil painting, the classic car in the garage or coin collections. Just avoid locking eyes with the enemy.

Keep Moving Around

In crowded settings, it is harder to notice people that are on the move. Casually walk around; explore the entire location, both inside and outside. Walk as though you have a purpose, as if you know where you are going. Avoid deep meaningful discussions. If you are engaged, redirect questions into small talk and keep moving. Most guests will be so busy doing their own thing; they won't notice your purposeful wandering.

Act Confidently

You can act with confidence without actually being confident. Do so by keeping your chin up, throwing your shoulders back, keeping your arms loose, relaxing your demeanor and smiling. Under normal circumstances, you should make eye contact and engage in conversation. But don't do those things here. Don't overstate your confidence. Just appear comfortable with yourself and in your surroundings.

Consider What People Expect

Being self-aware goes a long way. Imagine how you appear to guests. Use that information to make adjustments in your attire and behavior to remain neutral. Focus comments on the event when engaged in conversations. Be agreeable, even if doing so means taking a position you despise. This is not the time to win new friends, a beauty contest, or a debate.

* * *

Case Notes

THE SINISTER MINISTER

AFTER THEIR YOUNGEST CHILD LEFT home, Mom and Dad adjusted well to their empty nest; by some accounts a little too well. Dad retired from his job as an aerospace engineer, and they traveled the country by RV. They were open and carefree, like college coeds experiencing independence for the first time. They visited national monuments, great lakes, and homes of their children and grandchildren along the way. Then suddenly while eating dinner with their daughter in Seattle, everything changed. Dad suffered a stroke and died.

The children took turns staying with Mom as she grieved. After a few months, they began resuming their day-to-day lives, raising their own children. Sad, depressed, and lonely, Mom turned to the bottle. In a matter of weeks, the sweet grandmother became a bitter, nasty drunk. She refused help and seemed set on destroying her family by spreading rumors of infidelity between her children's spouses. Vodka was her escape. Unfortunately, it was also the hammer that pounded wedges between Mom and her children. In a desperate attempt to protect their families, the children stopped talking to their mother and eventually to each other.

After two years of Alcoholics Anonymous meetings, Mom's depression improved. She used the proceeds from the sale of the family home and RV to purchase a smaller house in a nearby city. She also started attending a backyard church run by her nephew James, a self-proclaimed minister.

Mom was turning her life around and ready to reconcile with her beloved children. She told James everything that had happened, including how she chased her kids away with vicious rumors. With a minister's charm, James offered to help Mom through counseling and prayer. He promised to invite her children to reunification therapy. Mom was excited about being together with her children and grandchildren. She told James she'd do anything to restore those relationships.

Mom became an official member of Jame's church. She followed instructions to complete a registration card, provide income and asset disclosures and to sign a written promise to tithe 10% of her retirement income.

James made Mom's counseling his top priority. He also knew that Mom had $85,000 in her savings account. He received a deposit of $500 to start counseling, and asked for more money as they progressed. His promise to contact the kids at the right time kept Mom interested and open to paying higher counseling fees. Soon Mom was giving James $2,000 a month for "spiritual guidance" and contributing another $3,000 a month to his ministry. Although he never contacted the children, James led Mom to believe that he was counseling them separately and that they were not ready to begin conjoint therapy. Mom was watching her savings dwindle and knew she couldn't keep up with the costs. The lack of family contact caused her to slip into a deep state of depression. She was overcome with hopelessness. An entry from her diary stated, "Each passing day without contact from my children feels like a step closer to Hell."

Meeting with James no longer helped. He wasn't a licensed therapist and was woefully unqualified to treat Mom's depression. Mom started talking about suicide during her counseling sessions. James responded as any perfectly corrupt minister would. He went online and found a trust drafting service to create a trust on Mom's behalf. He filled out the trust questionnaire and gave each of Mom's children $10,000 and himself the balance of her estate totaling $350,000. He printed the trust and presented it to Mom for executing during a therapy session. She signed it as instructed.

James wasn't finished. After Mom signed the trust, he drove her to a funeral home—owned by his friend—and instructed her to participate in preneed funeral planning. She trusted James; he was the only blood relative within her social circle. She purchased her casket and burial plot as suggested. A week later, Mom was found dead with three empty bottles of Smirnoff on the floor next to her cold remains. The Coroner reported that she died from alcohol poising.. It was determined that she started binge drinking shortly after returning from the mortuary.

James had kept a little secret from Mom and each of her children. Before Mom came to his church, he knew the kids were searching for her. He was contacted by each of them separately. Mom was hard to find because after selling the family home, she didn't leave a forwarding address. James didn't help. In fact, he interfered by denying knowledge of her whereabouts. He claimed he hadn't seen her since Dad's death, and promised to pass on their messages if she came around.

James moved quickly to liquidate Mom's assets. He ignored his duty to give all of my children notice of his intent to administer her trust. Instead, he kept Mom's death a secret from them,sold her house and all her belongings, including family heirlooms. He took everything and acted like nothing happened.

Mom's daughter Victoria never stopped searching for her mother, though. Two months later, she discovered the news of her mother's death. Still unaware of James' involvement, she called to inform him of Mom's death and that she was going to open probate to take care of her estate. James had no choice. He admitted visiting Mom prior to her passing and being appointed as the trustee of her trust. Victoria was livid. She contacted her siblings, and they compared notes. Collectively they realized that James was keeping them apart from their mother. Soon thereafter, Victoria contacted my office for help.

We filed petitions with the probate court to stop James and to recover the assets he took. James had already used the proceeds from the sale of Mom's house to buy his own place. We moved quickly to get a court order forcing him to transfer his new house to Mom's trust. Victoria and her siblings are still suffering from the thought that they might have prevented Mom's suicide by responding to her addiction in a different manner.

STEP 5

CONTINUE MOVING TOWARDS HOME

"If you don't know where you're going you might end up somewhere else." ~ *Yogi Berra*

WITH A THREE STEP LEAD off third base, twist your back foot into the ground and remain balanced. As the pitcher raises his hands in a windup, start leaning towards home plate. Just before he releases the ball, explode off the start. Attack the ground in full force with each stride. Drive out so your body is at a 45-degree angle to the ground. Don't rise too quickly; let your body unfold naturally as you accelerate down the line. At this point there is no turning back.

When the window of opportunity opens, go through it quickly. Getting off to a strong start is necessary because things tighten up towards the end of your scam. Stay focused on your objectives. Be decisive in selecting the method. Complete each step. Then let your plan develop naturally. Don't rush; a small mistake at this stage will lead to failure.

CHAPTER EIGHT

SET CLEAR GOALS

SETTING GOALS IS THE BEST way to accomplish your scam. If you are thinking about stealing a home, bank accounts, a business, royalties, gold, diamonds, or an entire estate, now it's time to form a plan. It must be specific and realistic. If your goal is to take one of your mark's houses, narrow it down to something more specific. Do you want his primary residence or vacation home? Are you after the entire house or do you want a partial interest? Do you want it right now or later? Success is difficult to achieve without clear goals.

Goals Must be Attainable

You can accomplish almost any goal within the realm of possibility. . If you plan to acquire a house by tricking your mark into signing a transfer deed, make sure she is the sole owner. You should also confirm that she has the power and authority to execute a deed. If her ownership is limited to a joint tenant or if she's protected under a conservatorship, she lacks the legal ability to give you the house. That goal is unattainable. Do your research. Make sure success is possible before starting.

Setting goals for inheritance theft scams is a little different from most other pursuits because it typically involves taking assets by manipulating legal processes. You can take ownership of a car, boat, house, and other assets by transferring ownership of title. The transfer requires little more than the owner's signature. Here's where it gets thorny. Assets transferred into a trust are owned by the trust. The original owner loses ownership rights, including the authority to gift. The trust owns them upon receipt. Ownership rights transfer to the trustee and may be limited.. If your mark isn't a trustee, she lacks the authority to gift trust assets. Any attempts to do so can be easily set aside. Similarly, if your mark is a partial owner of real property, she lacks the ability to transfer the entire property; any attempt to do so can also be set aside with relative ease. If your goal involves taking tangible assets, start by identifying the person with both power and authority to make gifts. The following are tips should help..

How to Verify Ownership

Here are instructions for identifying owners of assets commonly taken by cons:

Real Estate. Ownership of real estate is verified by a title search. Start by obtaining the street address (or the assessor's parcel number or legal description, if possible) and the city and state of the subject property. Take that information to the County Recorder's or Treasurer's Office. Upon arrival, ask for help researching a property title. In most cases, you will be instructed on how to use a computerized county abstract system, which gives a property's ownership history. In some counties you can do this research online. You can also pay an online company, real estate agent or title company to pull title. It's best to do this yourself, however, to avoid leaving a witness trail.

Bank Accounts. Determining bank account ownership is easy because the owner's name is printed on the statements. If you have access to your mark's mail, you have the ability to locate her bank accounts. Pay particular attention to how bank statements are addressed. If the addressee is one person, then that person is the owner. If it is two people, then both may be owners with rights of survivorship. Sometimes the second name will be followed by the letters "WROS" or "WRS," meaning With Right of Survivorship. Accounts owned by trusts will be addressed to the trustee in a variety of different ways, such as:

- Jane Smith Trustee of
- The Smith Family Trust, utd 05/12/95
- Jane Smith TTEE
- Smith Family Trust
- utd 05/12/95
- Smith Family Trust
- FBO John Smith
- John Smith t/u/w
- John and Jane Smith t/u/a
- Robert Smith TTEE
- John Smith – t/u/w

Abbreviations:

- u/a—under agreement

- u/d/t—under deed of trust
- u/t/a—under trust agreement
- u/w/o—under will of
- ttee—trustee
- fbo—for benefit of

Any of these designations indicates that the account is owned by a trust. You must go through the trustee to take those assets.. There is another type of bank account ownership you should know about. If it is owned by a decedent's estate it will be addressed as follows:

- Jane Smith, Executor (or Administrator)
- Estate of Claudia R. Jones

Remember, before attempting to access a bank account you must identify the actual holder of the account. Do so by reviewing bank statements. Read them carefully to determine the holder's name. If an account is addressed to "Jane Smith's Trust," Jane Smith is not the owner. It is owned by Jane Smith's Trust and controlled by the trustee of that trust. If Jane Smith is the trustee, then "Jane Smith Trustee (TTEE)" is the only person with authority to access those funds. The same applies with Jane Smith as Executor of an estate. The proper title must be used in all transactions when applicable.

Brokerage (Investment) Accounts. Brokerage accounts are similar to bank accounts with one exception. Investment advisors are more likely to enjoy personal relationships with their clients. Ownership verification should be limited to reviewing statements mailed to your mark's house.

Life Insurance. Life insurance can be owned by the insured person, the beneficiary or a third party (such as a business or trust). Review the policy paperwork to verify ownership.

Precious Metals. Gold and silver coins and bars are not traceable. They are owned by whoever has the legal right of possession, including a trust. Defining the legal right of possession is somewhat complex, but in simple terms means having the exclusive use and custody of an item. The right of possession is a different legal concept than the right of property. For hard assets such as precious metals, jewelry, and art, the right of possession and right of property essentially mean the same thing. For property such as a house or car, however, the person who holds the right of property—the ultimate legal owner of the asset— may not be the same as the person who holds the right of possession— the person who legitimately occupies the house or drives the car.

Jewelry. Like precious metals, most items of jewelry are not traceable. They are also owned by whoever has the legal right of possession, including a trust.

Firearms. Ownership is determined by legal right of possession. It can sometimes be traced by purchase receipts.

Other Tangible Items. Similar to precious metals and jewelry, ownership of tangible personal property items (computers, stereo systems, cameras, paintings, collectible items, et cetera) is not usually determined by recorded title. Receipts, insurance inventories, and the like are often used to prove ownership, but absent such evidence, ownership is merely a concept. They go to whoever has the legal right of possession.

Small Businesses. Corporations are owned by their shareholders; sole-proprietorships are owned by individuals; limited liability companies (LLCs) can take on various forms of ownership; partnerships are owned by individual partners, who could include people or other business entities like partnerships, limited liability companies, and corporations. To determine ownership of a business, you will have to do significant research. Start by calling the business directly and asking, checking its website, searching the Better Business Bureau reports, searching your state's database of registered businesses, querying business information search engines and social networks, calling the local business licensing agency, and searching commercial websites offering business information for a fee. Also, if you have access, search the records of the business itself, especially its income tax returns.

Intangibles. Intangibles (excluding real estate and businesses) include other business-type assets that do not take a physical form, but have certain property rights and attributes that create value for their owners. They include intellectual property such as patents, trademarks, copyrights, and trade secrets. They also include mineral rights, oil and gas leases and royalties. Ownership of these rights is similar to ownership of tangible property. In most cases, intangible property rights are secured by documents issued by the United States Patent and Trademark Office, or through a contract. To find the owner, you must find the applicable paperwork.

Automobiles. Ownership of cars, trucks, boats, RVs, commercial vehicles, and motorcycles is determined by a Certificate of Title (commonly referred to as a pink slip). A copy is kept in the Department of Motor Vehicles database. The vehicle's registration will also contain information on the registered owner. It will show the name of the registered owner, or lienholder (the entity that holds the legal right of property) if the car is leased or being used as security for a loan.

Cash. Cash is essentially untraceable. It is owned by whoever has the legal right of possession, including a trust.

CHAPTER NINE

SCAM METHODS

IF YOU HAVE ALREADY SELECTED a mark, established a relationships, set attainable goals, and if the window of opportunity is open, then pick a scam method. There are several basic scam methods, and one emerging method called charity scams addressed in this chapter. Pick one that works well for your particular situation. Avoid the temptation of trying different methods hoping one might work. That is an excellent way of getting caught. You have come too far to get sloppy. Carefully select a method that meets your objectives.

Basic Scams

Misappropriation. This is the wrongful use of funds entrusted to you, but owned by someone else. It is commonly used by trustees of family trusts--people entrusted with care and management of trust assets after the settlor dies. Trustees have unfettered access and control over large amounts of money. What they do with it is another story.

The trick to misappropriation is avoiding detection. If you decide to take trust funds for personal use, be prepared to do some creative accounting. Hire an experienced forensic accountant willing to help you reconcile the "missing" trust assets.

Fraud. There are three types of fraud you should consider when using estate planning documents in your scam:

Fraud in the execution. Fraud in the execution occurs when you trick a mark into creating a will, trust, power of attorney, beneficiary designation, or any other estate planning type document that he believes reflects his will, but in reality reflects yours.

Fraud in the inducement. Fraud in the inducement occurs when you perpetrate a scam which directly affects the contents of your mark's will, trust, or estate plan. It includes, for example, a scam where you falsely accuse your brother of stealing your mother's wedding ring for the purpose of upsetting her to the point that she disinherits that son by removing him as a trust beneficiary.

Fraudulent prevention. This applies to the making or revocation of a will or trust. Fraudulent prevention involves acts designed to prevent someone from making, amending, or revoking a will or trust. It involves the intentional misrepresentation of laws or facts to stop another from acting on their desire to engage in estate planning activities. Telling your sick mother she can't add another beneficiary to her trust because she's too sick, when you know she can, is an example of fraudulent prevention.

False Billing. This is a fraudulent act of invoicing a mark for something they have no legal obligation to pay. You can use false billing in a few ways. You can invoice marks for things such as government services, internet fraud protection, magazine renewals, and so on. If they pay, you win. Not only do you pick up some spare change, you get your mark's name and credit card number which can be used to pull more lucrative scams. You can also use false billing practices to justify money you misappropriate from trusts or estates. Just use your imagination.

Fee Padding. Cons holding positions such as executors, trustees, conservators, and sales representatives can use this method against their marks. Fee padding is an act of adding excessive unearned charges to receipts. General contractors, for example, could target a senior for home repairs and then pad the bill with materials never used and unperformed services. Similarly, executors, trustees, and conservators can pad their time with false entries when accounting for their services to an estate or trust. Just make the additional goods or services appear reasonable under the circumstances. This is also an excellent way of reconciling misappropriated trust funds. Create fake receipts, or bribe third party service providers to create them for you in exchange for repeat business and cash payments.

Forgery of Documents. Forging documents with today's word processing technology is almost trivial. Wills and trusts are written with word processors, styled in common font faces and sizes. Replacing an original page with a forgery is easy. A trust can be altered, for example, by replacing the beneficiary identification page with a forgery naming you as the sole beneficiary. Just draft the page you're forging using the original document's fonts and format. Once you're finished, insert it in place of the original page. Yes, it's really that easy.

Forgery of Signature. Reproducing a mark's signature is a common inheritance theft strategy. Doing it right takes practice. Sign your mark's name several times until it looks similar to an original signature. Creating the perfect forgery is essentially impossible because experts can always find inconsistent pen lifts or pressure points. Strive to make it look good enough to discourage challenges. If your mark has Parkinson's disease or another neuromuscular disorder, her signature may appear shaky. That type of signature is difficult to forge. Instead, copy one made by your mark before she started trembling. You can find samples on old cards, letters and business correspondences. Some signatures must be witnessed by a notary public. If you can't obtain a false identification card to present to a notary, then find one who will notarize your signature without requiring identification. It may take a few more phone calls and a little extra money, but they are available for hire.

Identity Theft. Identity theft occurs when you steal someone's identity for the purpose of committing a crime. It requires the acquisition of enough information about your mark—such as their name, date of birth, Social Security number, and mailing address—that you can assume their identity. Criminals use identity theft to commit two different types of fraud, financial fraud and criminal activities fraud. You should only focus on financial fraud. Consider using your client's identity for any of the following scams:

- Bank fraud.
- Debit/Credit card fraud.
- Computer and telecommunications fraud.
- Social program fraud.
- Retirement fraud.
- Tax refund fraud.
- Mail fraud.

These methods are the safe because human contact is not required. Practice stealthy tactics to use your mark's personal information for as long as possible. Use different approaches to access his personal information. Hack his personal computer; dig through his trash for documents, mail, and discarded prescription bottles; steal confidential records from government, client, and employee files (this requires access); hack credit card terminal devices to capture debit/credit card numbers as they are processed (this requires special skills); lift a mark's wallet, handbag, or purse; steal bank and credit card statements, brokerage statements, new checks, and income tax information from the mail; submit a change of address form to divert his mail to another more convenient location; and steal personal information from his home.

You may also use the following social engineering methods to commit identity theft:

Pretexting. Obtaining your mark's private information by pretending to be someone else.

Phishing. Using spam email to direct your mark to a phony but legitimate-looking internet commerce site that you control.

Shoulder surfing. Obtaining your mark's personal information by watching him type personal information, such as pin numbers.

Sweet talking. Using friendly banter or gossip techniques to entice someone with access to your mark's personal information to share it with you.

Bribing. Paying a person in a position of trust for confidential information about your mark.

Eavesdropping. Obtain information by listening to your mark's private conversations.

Although there are many high-tech ways of stealing personal information, stealing wallets and dumpster diving are most effective. In other words, stick to the basics. Don't attempt something as complex as phishing marks without experience, especially when you can accomplish the same objective by simply borrowing your his wallet for a while.

Theft. This is simplest of all basic scam methods. You can steal from your mark directly, from her trust, or from her estate. All scams involve theft in one form or another. You can steal everything from shoes to mineral rights. Transferring assets from your mark's bank account to yours is a form a theft. Using your mark's power of attorney to convert her assets to your name and taking your grandmother's wedding ring are two more examples.

Skimming. This involves slowly taking money from income-producing assets. If your mark has an income-producing asset, such as rental property, skimming from rents collected is a good way of taking money without drawing too much attention to yourself. The trustee of a trust can do very well by skimming rent from trust rental property, especially if the trustee has the power to raise rents without the mark's knowledge.

Coercion. Coercion scams involve the acquisition of assets by intimidating your mark to do something against his will. Use psychological pressure, physical force, or threats. This can be extremely effective if your mark is struggling with mental capacity issues and fears losing his independence. If your mark values his independence, the mere threat of reporting him "to the authorities" for placement in an "old-folks home" could compel an amendment his estate plan in your favor. It is a cruel strategy, but highly effective.

Undue Influence. This is perhaps the most used of all basic scam methods. It works by pressuring your mark to execute a will or trust reflecting your wishes. You can also use it to force him to make a gift or to sign a contract. The pressure must be so great that he loses the ability to exercise independent judgment. It is similar to coercion, but differs in the techniques applied. Where coercion uses threats, this method requires the application of exhortation, insinuation, flattery, trickery, and deception. Use urgency persistence and unrelenting pressure in your demands. Undue influence is most effective with marks susceptible to manipulation due to mental, psychological, or physical disabilities. It is especially effective on marks dependent on your company. If you use this method, consider the following tips:

- Aggressively initiate the transaction.
- Isolate your mark from outsiders.
- Discourage him from seeking independent advice.
- Charity Scams: Gift Cultivation and Solicitation

Gift cultivation and solicitation processes are regularly used by respectable organizations engaged in legitimate fundraising activities. Hospitals, universities, and religious organizations have raised billions of dollars with this technique. Don't reinvent the wheel; if you're considering this scam method, copy their model.

To start, you will need to create a charity designed to serve a public interest. It must be organized and operated for an exempt purpose under Internal Revenue Code section 501(c)(3). There are other requirements for getting tax exempt status. Do good research before selecting this scam method. Creating a fictitious charity to solicit contributions from several marks over a period of years takes commitment of time, money, and energy. It's also very risky. While there is nothing illegal about soliciting contributions for charitable causes, creating a fictitious charity as a front for your inheritance theft scam is the type of fraud that can land you in prison.

Once you establish an "exempt organization," use the following seven-step cycle to rake in the money:

- Identifying your mark.
- Researching your mark.
- Strategic planning.
- Cultivation.
- Solicitation.
- Stewardship.
- Renewal.

Let's go over each step in more detail.

Step one: Identify your Mark:

Find people who are empathetic to the purpose of your fictitious charity and that have the ability to make satisfying gifts. If your gaze is already fixed on the perfect mark, create a charity that she would support. Then build your base of like-minded supporters (marks) from that point. Alternately, you might want to create a charity that appeals to your targets in general before selecting marks.

Step two: Research your Mark

This is an extension of the identification process. Research involves understanding the motivations and interests of your mark, in order to ascertain what factors may lead them towards gift-giving. Some information may be in public records. Your mark may already support similar philanthropic enterprises. Her name may already be etched on donor plaques inside buildings. The research may include estimating your mark's net worth by doing an asset search, or hiring a private investigator to do it for you.

The best information will come through personal contact. Engage in conversations that elicit insight into your mark's priorities, personal beliefs, and charitable objectives. It takes skill, sensitivity, and patience. Before someone is motivated to give and or disclose potential gifting criteria, they must trust you. Most people only open up after several interactions. Get answers to as many of the following questions as possible:

- What is your mark's greatest accomplishment?
- What are your mark's goals for retirement?
- What does your mark want to leave as her legacy?
- What does your mark think of your "charity?"
- Does your mark have any opinions about your "charity's" mission?
- Who in your mark's family and circle of advisors does she consult before giving?
- Does your mark want to pass assets along to children or grandchildren?

Keep a file of information on all potential marks. Update those files as new or additional information becomes available.

Step three: Strategic Planning

Treat each mark as if they have advisors; people who are in a position to formulate the size, shape, and timing of a contribution. Learn their names, interests, and criteria for charitable gifting.

Understand that gifting is tangible evidence of an emotional event. A gift is a voluntary action; it is not a payment for service, or an obligation. It is given freely by marks attempting to satisfy certain spiritual, emotional, or personal objectives. Your job is to create opportunities for your mark to attain those objectives through gifting. After receiving contributions, convince donors that your "charity" is rendering the works for which the gift was solicited. This can be a little challenging since your "charity's" true purpose is to line your pockets.

Part of your plan should include finding ways to involve marks in your operation. You will receive larger contributions from marks who are actively engaged in the charity's growth, through solicitation, promotion or management. Since giving is something that comes from the heart, connect with your mark's emotions and illustrate how their contributions have a meaningful impact on the lives of others. Finally, provide opportunities for awards and community recognition, especially when it involves their personal contributions outside of writing checks.

There is a dynamic tension between planning and execution. Don't hide behind the planning process waiting for more information before stepping from behind the desk. You can fine-tune your plan ad infinitum, but if until you start cultivating marks you will miss opportunities for major contributions. On the other hand, if you ask for a gift before considering your mark's needs, interests, or history, anything you receive will likely be less than what your mark would have given under the right circumstances. Either a rushed act or an outright inaction can lead to the same result—no gift.

Step four: Cultivation

This is a process of informing marks about your (fictitious) organization, its leadership, its vision for the future, and its value. This process can take from six to 24 months and require a series of eight to 10 contacts over that period.

The final stage of cultivation occurs when your mark realizes that the two of you have a common vision, that your leadership is exemplary, that you have the ability to deliver the vision and that the only thing standing in the way of success is the lack of money—which your mark has. The mark's gift becomes a natural resolution to a mutually recognized problem.

The cultivation stage is complete when your marks gifts assets without hesitation. The mark should feel that gifting is her idea. Cultivation is a two-way street. You need to know your mark just as she needs to know you. You may discover during the course of cultivation that although she has the resources to give, you are not in a position to do the works in which she is interested. If there is no connection between your mark's interest and your "charitable" works, there will be no gift. So do good research before cultivating your mark.

Your mark may want to examine your organization in detail before gifting. She may ask to see a copy of your annual report, list of trustees, and endowment performance. Be prepared to handle such requests expeditiously and, since you likely won't have that information, diplomatically. If you can't come up with reasonable responses for a persistent mark, it may be best to move on. Otherwise keep your marks happy and satisfied.

Act as if your "charity" does not have needs. Treat your marks as having needs and your charity as an opportunity for meeting them. Gently embrace those points to create a sense of dependency.

Step five: Solicitation

This involves four parts, and will almost certainly take place in a face-to-face setting.

State your case. Tell your mark you are there to ask for a meaningful gift in support of works in which you both share a common interest. Tell them what you plan to accomplish, how you intend to finance it, how you will monitor its progress, and what you would like them to do. The "works", of course, are never actually completed as promised.

Listen. Learn how to become an active listener. Listen to your mark's voice. Interpret her facial expressions and body language. Hear what she is telling you—and not telling you—about her interests, her capacity, and the timing of your request. Once you have stated your case, let her respond. You are soliciting her donation, so don't fill the air with the sound of your voice. Be flattering by showing interest in the sound of hers.

Ask for the gift. Practice stating, "Will you consider a gift of $100,000?" Then stop talking and wait for her response. The amount of your request will change depending on your mark's charitable habits and gifting abilities.

Say thank you. Say thank you regardless of her response.

Step six: Stewardship

It is crucial that your marks know how their gifts were used. Inform them of your organization's success in completing the works for which you solicited the gift. If the gift created an endowment for education, introduce your mark to someone pretending to be a student benefitting from the fund.

Find innovative ways to maintain ongoing discussions about the progress made by your fictitious charity with each of your marks. Don't just accept gifts and move on to something else. Keep your marks close. Published research has shown that word of mouth advertising is far more effective in attracting new business than purchased advertising. The last thing you want is a mark telling other potential marks that she was forgotten after writing a check.

Stewardship involves the wise use of money and the proper delivery of services. Make certain that you have the accounting practices in place to assure marks that their money cannot be siphoned off, embezzled, or poorly managed. Your marks should think that you do everything well, including money management. If they know you're a poor money manager, find someone to do it for you.

Note, savvy cons can turn even an apparent flaw like a reputation for poor money management into a benefit. Remember the lesson about always telling the truth, even if it hurts a little? Acknowledging past financial mistakes and preventing similar mistakes in the future by hiring a creditable accounting firm, creates the illusion of honest self-awareness.

Step seven: Renewal

This step involves resuming the gift cultivation process. It's no secret that marketing strategies designed to generate repeat gifting from the same mark are more efficient than those intended to produce gifts from new marks. Your renewal challenges are twofold. They include turning first time contributors into repeat gift makers, and then into loyal promoters of your organization. Marks become repeat gift makers if they feel connected to an important aspect of your organization. Implement systems encouraging multiple contributions as part of your organization's culture. Offer them exclusive admission to special events, send them birthday and anniversary cards, and memorialize their gifts by including their names on donor plaques displayed in public view. Involve them in the organization's success by inviting them to chair a committee or to serve on your board of directors.

Ask for their continued support by referring other marks. They have already proven their commitment by gifting; if treated with continual respect and appreciation, they will give again. But don't stop there. Leverage your relationship by asking them if they can help you solicit donations from other marks. Loyal contributors can be very effective recruiters. They may socialize with people who share similar beliefs and have similar assets. Stewardship leads to renewal that leads to identification of more marks, and that leads to a new gift cultivation and solicitation cycle.

Scam Method Selection

Use the following approach to identify the best scam method for your situation:

- List your scam goals.
- Identify potential scam methods.
- Test the feasibility of each method by applying them to the known facts and circumstances of your situation.
- Choose the most suitable method or combination of methods.

Here is an example of this approach:

Problem Statement

In this scenario our mark is the Sanchez Family Trust. The trust was set up by an 84-year-old divorced woman named Rosa Sanchez (the settlor). It was funded with a $375,000 house (by deed), $200,000 in various financial accounts (by title) and $50,000 in gold bars (by declaration). Rosa's social circle of family and friends includes two children in their early 60s, a CPA who also serves as her financial advisor, a friend named Margret whom she has known for nearly 40 years, and two very close neighbors. Her oldest son Hector is the successor trustee of the trust, meaning that he will become the trust's manager when Rosa is no longer capable of performing her trustee duties. Rosa has dementia, but refuses to see a doctor in fear that a formal diagnosis could lead to the loss of her independence. Other than that, she is in pretty good health. What scam method, or combinations of methods, should be used to immediately take all trust assets?

Solution

Finding the best scam method is a four-step process. Let's work through each step:

List goals. Here are the goals: 1) Take all assets in the Sanchez Family Trust. 2) Take them immediately.

Identify potential scam methods. You should always test a variety of scam methods. But, for purposes of this example, we only tested two. We compared the effectiveness of amending the trust's terms with stealing assets directly from the trust.

Test methods. A key part of the analysis is to test each potential scam method's probability of success. That can be accomplished by applying various scam methods to the facts and circumstances of your mark's situation. For example:

Amending Trust Terms: Amending the trust's terms could be a good way of eventually owning all of its assets (assuming the amendment can survive a vigorous legal challenge) but because trust assets are distributed after the settlor (owner of the trust) passes-away, it is not the fastest way to take possession of assets. This method would keep you from meeting the goal of taking possession of the assets as soon as possible.

Stealing From The Trust: You can take assets directly from the trust in a variety of ways. For assets requiring deed or title for ownership, we would have to either trick Rosa (in her capacity as trustee) into signing her name on transfer documents or duplicate her signature by forgery. You can take ownership of the house by simply signing Rosa's name on a grant deed. But that is not enough to meet our goal of actual possession. Once the grant deed is recorded you could initiate legal action to take possession, such as pushing Rosa into a senior living facility or retaining an attorney to evict her from the house. The risk of detection is high, but for purposes of this example minimizing risk of detection is not one of our goals. As such this method is still viable. Taking the financial accounts is easier. You can become a joint holder on those accounts with a simple signature. Stealing the gold bars would be easiest because possession determines ownership. Just take them from the house.

Choose the best method. In this example it is possible to take all the trust assets using either method. The biggest difference is that you can gain possession faster by stealing assets separately out of the trust. Since immediate possession is one of our two goals, the scam method of stealing each asset separately is the best choice.

CHAPTER TEN

USING INSTRUMENTS

THERE ARE MANY WAYS TO covertly acquire legal possession of your mark's assets. In this chapter you will learn to pull scams using instruments—a fancy word for legal documents of various forms. These types of scams are favored because they require little effort and produce great results. They involve creating ownership interest in your marks assets using power of attorney forms, grant deeds, wills, trusts and payment on death beneficiary designations. They are the means by which legal ownership is transferred between people in ordinary circumstances, and are easy to exploit.. Transfers made with these instruments are rarely noticed until your mark dies. If you use this method, your mark's death will trigger subsequent action to complete the scam. Act quickly before beneficiaries hire an attorney to freeze assets. The top five instruments favored by cons are as follows:

Power of Attorney. Powers of attorney for financial management are included in estate plans for the purpose of transferring decision making authority from the "Principal" to the designated "Agent" upon the Principal's incapacity or other triggering event such as when the principal leaves the country.. They are different from conservatorship powers because they can be created outside of court, and the principal must be of sound mind at the time of execution. They typically give an agent authority over a very broad scope of financial activities, including the power to receive income, pay bills, invest assets, borrow money, lend money, sell assets, collect debts, and pursue legal actions. An agent usually has a great deal of decision-making authority over the principal's assets. Agents also have full access to checking and savings accounts, brokerage accounts, and all income streams. An agent's activity is not formally supervised, but overt and careless actions could draw third party scrutiny. A power of attorney for financial management can only be used during the principal's life.

Real Property Grant Deeds. Real property grant deeds are used to transfer real property ownership from one person to another. They are useful for transferring real estate outright to a trust, to another individual, or to create joint tenancy interest. Compel your mark into using a grant deed to convey real property from themselves as individuals to themselves and you as joint tenants. Ownership will remain with the mark during their life and quietly transfer to you upon their death by operation of law (outside probate or trust administration).

Last Will and Testament. Most wills require signatures from two independent witnesses. I am going to tell you about a type of will that is equally effective, but doesn't require witnesses. It's called a holographic will. It's simply a testament that is entirely handwritten and signed by the testator (person writing the will). Holographic wills are very simple in form. If your mark wrote, "Upon my death my buddy Ron Sampson shall receive my Beverly Hills mansion" on a cocktail napkin and signed his name, the napkin would qualify as a holographic will. It could be offered to open probate on your mark's estate. That cocktail napkin is all that Ron needs to inherit the mansion. Isn't this fun!

Family Trusts. It seems like everyone has a trust, and why not? They are very useful for transferring assets outside of probate court. Like a standard will, they must be witnessed but not notarized. They may also be amended and there is no limited to the number of amendments the settlor (person making the trust) can make. Your real opportunity comes in creating amendments.

Trusts can be amended without involving anyone other than the settlor. The amendment process can differ from trust to trust and is usually spelled out in the original trust instrument. Most of the time an amendment only requires the settlor to sign a written document describing the substance of the amendment. Amendments are not limited to asset distributions. Successor trustees can be changed, immediate gifts can be made and beneficiaries can be added or deleted. They can be used to completely revoke and rewrite any of the original trust provisions. Trusts are favored because they are privately administered, that also makes them vulnerable to scams.

Beneficiary Designations. Bank accounts, brokerage accounts, life insurance policies, pensions, 401Ks, certificates of deposit, and a host of other financial instruments have beneficiary designation options. Those designations can be made or changed by filling out a simple postcard. Assets with beneficiary designations transfer to the designated beneficiary directly upon the death of the owner, outside of probate and trust administration. They transfer directly to the designated beneficiary without notice to heirs upon verification of the principal's death and proof of the designated beneficiary's identity.

CHAPTER ELEVEN

GO, GO, GO ... RUN HARD!

ONCE YOU COMMIT TO STEALING from your mark don't look back., Stay focused on the step in front of you and charge ahead. Replace any negative thoughts with positive affirmations. Tell yourself, "I deserve to have and enjoy prosperity." Think about how having money will improve your life. If it's a home you're after, visualize yourself comfortably reclining in the living room watching your favorite movie. You can't publically proclaim these goals. So use the power of positive thinking to propel action.

Consider the following tips when your scam method involves the use of documents:

Obtaining Instruments

Estate planning instruments are easy to find. You can get them from estate planning attorneys, title companies, financial institutions, books, office supply stores, and online.

Going to an attorney is a high-risk, high-reward proposition, but you should never consider doing it unless you control your mark or the attorney. I handled one case where a con contacted an attorney in another county, pretended to be the mark and had the attorney prepare a trust without ever visiting the office. All communications were made by e-mail and telephone. Once completed the trust was sent to the con by mail. Attorney-prepared estate plans are more likely to withstand court challenges. However, attorneys are also aware of inheritance theft scams, so if you get caught they can be used as witnesses against you during trial.

If your scam involves adding yourself to a real estate deed, you can contact a title company to prepare the deed for you. Again, when you involve outsiders, use caution. If they smell a rat, they could turn quickly. Blank grant deed forms are easy to find and execute. The same can be said for changing bank account beneficiary designations. The forms can be obtained from your mark's financial institution. Most of them will even send them out by mail.

There are numerous online sources selling the instruments you need. Many of them will let you prepare wills, trusts, beneficiary designations, grant deeds, and just about anything else you might want. Typically, you complete an online questionnaire, and the instrument will be sent to you by mail or immediate download with instructions for final execution and recordation.

Start Executing the Instruments

Give the prepared instrument to your mark for execution. You should be very careful in your approach. Present it when she is tired, confused or disoriented. Do not let her hold on to it for review at a later time.. Give a general explanation how it benefits her and why it requires immediate attention. If she is reluctant to cooperate, pay a loyal friend to pose as an attorney. Have him come to the house and handle the execution process.

Finding Witnesses

If the instrument requires witnesses, you should already have a few people in mind. Look for someone passive and non-confrontational. Stay away from anyone willing to offer unsolicited opinions. Do not use anyone, including yourself, who could receive anything from the instrument.

Forge Your Mark's Name

If your scam involves the forgery of an instrument, then do so with the expectation that it will be challenged. Collect as many copies of your mark's signature as possible. If you have possession of all the known samples of her signature, challengers will have difficulty because their expert will lack sufficient signature samples for making a creditable analysis. Take possession of driver's license, credit cards, contracts, cards, letters, loan documents, and anything else containing your mark's handwriting or signature.

A complete lack of known samples may also arouse suspicion so replace some of those samples with matching forgeries. Contracts, which should have the signatures as the only handwriting on them, are a possibility. You may have to forge other parties' signatures as well, but those signatures won't be the ones under challenge in court. Personal letters, especially if you can find a stock of vintage stationery, are another good option. Copy them out from the ones you have stolen, supplying your forged signature at the end.

Notary For Hire

If you intend to record the instrument at the county recorder's office it must be notarized by a notary public. You should also consider having trust documents notarized because doing so adds a degree of authenticity. A notary can only notarize the signature of someone they know personally or who can verify their identification—usually with a driver's license. A few years ago I accepted a case where a certified notary public verified the signature of a man that lacked the ability to write. The notary was either bribed or the con obtained a fake identification card.

* * *

Case Notes

CAGEY CAREGIVER

DURING AN OFFICE CONSULTATION JOSH said that Caregiver took $180,000 from his father's savings account at Farmers & Merchants Bank. He vacillated between disbelief and denial while explaining how easy it is to become the beneficiary of a bank account. "My father signed a new beneficiary designation card, listing her as the sole beneficiary of that account." "There's no way he understood the consequences." "How could the Bank let that happen?"

Paul was a widower of about 2 years when he lost the ability to take care of himself. Josh exercised authority as agent under power of attorney agent to hire Caregiver. Caregiver was on time and in charge. She improved Paul's quality of life. She cooked, cleaned, bathed, fed and pampered him like a dependent child.

I explained that cons sometimes build strong bonds with marks for the purpose of using threats of abandonment to compel their cooperation. It seems as though the Caregiver got Paul's signature by exploiting his insecurity, when he was most susceptible to her will. The banks don't let those things happen, they work hard to prevent fraud. In happens because con's have the upper hand on unsuspecting people. They know how to gain trust and work systems.

Josh understood the need to work fast. We filed a petition to set-aside that beneficiary designation card and requested an emergency hearing to secure those funds pending trial. The court ordered Caregiver to deposit the entire $180,000 in a blocked account within 2 days--she was also ordered to file proof of compliance within 7 days. Caregiver's attorney filed a response denying the allegations.

We immediately hired an expert witness to conduct a retrospective evaluation of Paul's mental condition at the time he signed the card. After reviewing medical and factual evidence, our expert concluded with a high degree of confidence that Paul was infirm, depended and susceptible to undue influence. We attached the report as an exhibit to a letter outlining our legal arguments and proposing an immediate 15/85 settlement. Within three days, Caregiver countered with a 20/80 offer. In accepting the offer, Josh reasoned that receiving a net of roughly $130,000 was better than spending an additional $25,000 to $50,000 in attorney fees and costs for a chance at $180,000.

STEP 6

AVOID THE TAG

"This game isn't over till it's over." ~ *Yogi Berra*

DURING THE FIRST GAME OF the 1955 World Series between the Dodgers and Yankees, Jackie Robinson stole home in the 9th inning against pitcher Whitey Ford. He slid into home plate under Yogi Berra's glove.. Avoiding the tag is essential to your success too. If your actions are ever questioned, take immediate steps to divert attention. If that fails, execute your defense strategy. The following tips will help you score even if everyone sees you coming.

CHAPTER TWELVE

COVER YOUR TRACKS

THE MAIN ADVANTAGE YOU HAVE over beneficiaries is your access to, and control of, information. You should have possession of the instruments and documents used in your scam. Beneficiaries usually have nothing, sometimes not even a copy of the most current estate plan. The way you manage that information could be the difference between partial success and complete failure. Take the following action to manage damage control after detection.

Hide Documents

Experienced probate litigators dig deep to find documents. They even hire forensic computer technicians to retrieve information from your computer, outside email, the cloud and other electronic devices. You must Scrub your computer's hard drive of evidence connecting you to a scam. Don't do this alone. Contact an experienced computer technician. You might even consider replacing your computer's hard drive altogether. Keep hard copies of essential documents in a hidden safe. Don't use safe deposit boxes because banks can be ordered to deliver their contents to your opposition.

Keep the Peace

When communicating with people affected by your scam, especially if they are family members, keep the peace by choosing your words that reflect empathy, understanding and agreement, while dodging their questions. Treat any unsolicited advice, on something like how to administer the trust more quickly by saying "Thank you, I'll try to do that." When confronted by anger, respond with, "Why don't we start by listing the facts." Then ask for more time to do more research. If a discussion starts to get heated, stop it immediately. Say something like, "Let's wait on this until we have more information." Tough questions can be managed by stating, "You're entitled to accurate information, let me check into it. I'll get back to you with an answer next week."

Foster Delay

Don't start flexing your muscles now. You may have taken control over your mark's trust or the legal title to her home, but flaunting your success directly or indirectly will draw unwanted attention. Act dignified. Be confident, but tight-lipped. The longer you keep beneficiaries guessing about their inheritance, the better your chances of pulling off the scam. If you make them angry, they will hire an attorney. You need to buy time. Pretend everything is going as expected. If your scam involves your role as trustee of a trust, tell them you are interviewing attorneys to assist you with the administration process. Perform your duties well. Don't give them a reason to have you removed. After you hire an attorney, blame him for any further delays. Consider moving to another state. Redirect inquires. If possible use your mark as a shield. Screen telephone calls, and wait to return them until after you've thought of a good answer. Do whatever it takes to peacefully create delay.

CHAPTER THIRTEEN

KILLER ATTOURNEY FEE STRATEGIES

IN CHAPTER ONE, YOU WERE advised against stealing home in the first inning of a ball game. But now is different. You are into the final innings of play; it's time to pull out all the stops. At this point, you've decided to steal home, but perhaps you didn't play it as well as you should have and it appears that beneficiaries are going to sue. Don't worry. I anticipated your mistake and came up with a trick play to get you home safely. Just put aside some of your mark's money to hire an attorney for your defense. If you can't, there are other options. So keep going, run hard, and whatever you do, don't look back!

Use Your Mark's Money

If your mark is an infirm benefactor and your scam method involves coercion, undue influence, fraud, or the exploitation of diminished mental capacity, then simply ask your mark to set aside funds to cover possible legal expenses. You will be surprised how quickly some marks jump at the opportunity to defend their actions, eager to show that they are still in control. Ask them to add you as a joint holder of their checking and savings accounts, to set aside cash, to add you as a beneficiary of their life insurance, 401k or brokerage account. Use your imagination, but make sure the legal defense funds are available to you as needed.

Use Trust Funds

If you are the successor trustee of a trust funded with cash assets, then you're in a very good position. Most trusts give successor trustees the authority to use trust funds to defend the trust. If the instrument of your scam involves a trust, you have the "authority" to use those funds to defend the trust. That includes using the funds to block attempts to remove you as trustee. From a legal perspective, there is a fine line between defending the trust and defending yourself personally for breaching your duties as trustee. If you are accused of breaching your duties, the court will most likely suspend your power to pay attorney fees from the trust. However, courts rarely suspend trustee powers without a hearing, so talk to your attorney about pre-funding your legal defense with trust assets before the court makes any orders.

Use Estate Funds

If your scam involves a will you will need to hire a probate attorney. Probate attorneys are paid at the close of probate from estate funds. You do not have to use any of your money, except for a filing fee and other nominal costs for administrative services. Most probate attorneys want some money up front to cover those ordinary probate costs. Once your mark's will is offered to probate, notice is given to all heirs. If any of them contest the will, your attorney may require that you to enter into another fee agreement to handle the will contest. Consider asking your attorney to handle the will contest on a contingency fee basis. If they decline, you will likely have to pay some sort of a retainer at that time. If nobody contests the will, but later contests your actions as executor, you can once again use estate funds to defend those actions.

The Nuclear Option

A common and very effective strategy to ward off aggressive beneficiaries is to threaten the use of their inheritance to fund expensive litigation. It will help you retain control because most people hate the idea of watching their inheritance go to attorneys. They would rather risk losing it to you than see it go to litigation attorneys set on protecting your interests. Once you hire an attorney, the beneficiaries will likely hire one as well, and very few beneficiaries want to go down that path. Use the nuclear option to buy the time you need to finish your scam.

* * *

Case Notes

HOMELESS HARRY

OUR RECEPTIONIST, RENE, SAID THERE was a man in the lobby asking for me. I quickly checked my calendar, thinking I might have forgotten an appointment. "There's nothing else set for this afternoon," I responded. "I know," she replied, "he just walked into the office."

We typically don't take appointments on demand, but my calendar was clear and I was curious. Upon opening the lobby door, I saw a man sitting comfortably with his legs crossed, reading a magazine. His thin frame was draped with old, faded, dirty, and oversized clothes. The entire lobby reeked of pungent body odor and a warm, fruity, alcoholic beverage. The man was clearly homeless. We locked eyes as he rose to shake hands. "I am Harry," he said bluntly.

He gripped my hand with the confidence of an executive. His station in life certainly wasn't going to get in his way today. He had a sense of purpose. I motioned him toward an empty conference room. The smell was nearly intolerable. Yet, there was something intriguing about Harry. There was a well-adjusted man hidden beneath the distracting exterior, one that likely surfaced only on rare occasions. Today was important to Harry, it was a rare occasion—he was mentally sharp, and despite the strong smells, surprisingly coherent.

With little prompting, Harry went right into the purpose of his visit. He said his parents had both passed away—first his father, and about a year later, his mother. They left two children, himself, and his older brother, Frank. His parents' estate consisted of a duplex valued at $425,000, but nothing else of value. His father became sick several years ago. Shortly after he was admitted to the hospital, Frank took charge. Frank moved into the back unit of the duplex with his mother and rented the front unit to a young family. His father had been bedridden in the Veterans Administration Hospital for eight years prior to his passing. He suffered from severe osteoarthritis. According to Harry, his father's condition was so bad his hands were permanently curled inward, and his arms immobile.

Harry said he needed our help because his mother had recently passed away and Frank had taken the duplex for himself. He handed me a power of attorney for his father. I quickly reviewed it and noticed that Frank was the agent and that the father's name was signed in beautiful cursive writing. Harry said it didn't look like his father's signature, and that his father couldn't have signed it because he couldn't use his hands. He then handed me the trust. Again I quickly reviewed it and noticed that Frank was the sole beneficiary. Harry said that Frank used the power to create a family trust and to transfer title of the duplex from his parents to the trust. Harry was upset because he felt cheated by Frank. His parents had always promised to give the duplex to both of them equally.

Harry was more organized than most clients with scheduled appointments. He had everything in a tabulated folder, including a copy of his father's death certificate. He repeatedly pointed out that his father couldn't have signed the power of attorney because his hands were unusable. Harry was right. The signature looked perfect. How could someone in his father's condition scribe such a beautiful signature? I agreed to take the case.

While reviewing the power of attorney signature page, I found another irregularity. The power of attorney was notarized by an advocate at the VA Hospital. If Harry's father truly lacked the ability to sign, whose signature was on the instrument? How did they get that past the VA Hospital advocate? I assured Harry we would do our best to make it right. A few days later, while reviewing the power of attorney in more detail, I discovered that it did not give Frank the power to create a trust for his father. As a result, I knew we could set aside the trust and put the house in probate—which would give Harry his equal interest.

We tried to settle with Frank, but he insisted on having his day in court. While preparing for trial, we obtained bank statements showing that Frank had been stealing his parents' Social Security checks for nearly eight years. We also had Frank's bank statements. They contained over one hundred deposit entries from rents he collected on his parent's duplex. The stolen money, plus interest, attorney fees and costs exceeded Frank's share of his mother's estate.

On the day of trial, Frank appeared in court without an attorney. Harry offered him $40,000 from the $425,000 estate to settle. Frank suddenly realized he would get nothing if it went to trial and quickly accepted the offer. Upon hearing of the agreement, the trial judge was not pleased. He initially denied the settlement, saying he didn't think Frank should receive anything from the estate. Personally, I agreed with the judge. But Harry told the judge that Frank was still his brother and that he wished to uphold his parents' wishes by giving him something. The judge approved the settlement, and Harry and Frank left the courthouse together.

AFTERWORD

WHEN THE ELDERLY BECOME VULNERABLE due to declining physical and mental health, the threat of inheritance theft becomes all too real. This book is a result of my participation in hundreds of contested estate and trust matters during the past 18 years, bearing witness to the damage done to families from all walks of life. It is my hope that this volume raises the public's awareness of inheritance theft, not only in Southern California where I practice, but across the country.

BIBLIOGRAPHY

"Complacency." Grey Owl Avaition Consultants, Inc. Greyowl. com (May 2011) <http://www.greyowl.com/articles/complac_ article.pdf>

Contributor. *"How to Steal Home."* eHow.com (January 2010) <http://www.ehow.com/how_2058580_steal-home.html>

Csays, Jimmy. *"The New York Times and a young Sulzberger stake a claim in Kansas City."* At the juncture of journalism and daily life in Kansas City. JimmyCsays.com (September 20, 2010) <http://jimmycsays.com>

Freedman, Russell. Children of the Great Depression. *New York, NY: Clarion Books* (2005)

Grindley, Klye (and 13 others). *"How to Avoid Attention,"* Wikihow.com (March 2010) <http://www.wikihow.com/Avoid-Attention>

Guliuzza, P.E., M.D., Randy J. *"Darwin's Sacred Imposter: Recognizing Missed Warning Signs"* Acts & Facts. 40 (5): 12-15. (2011)

Halttunen, Karen. Confidence Men and Painted Women. *Yale University Press.* (1986)

Henderson, Les. Crimes of Persuasion, Schemes, Scams, Frauds. *Coyote Ridge Publishing*, 2nd edition (2003)

Hodge, James M. *"Gifts of Significance."* Increasing the Understanding of Philanthropy and Improving its Practice. *The Center on Philanthropy, at Indiana University.* (April 2011) <http://www.philanthropy.iupui.edu/TheFundRaisingSchool/PrecourseReadings/precourse_giftsofsignificancehodge.aspx>

Hudson, Shane. *"Maslow's Hierarchy of Needs, Success Circuit,"* (February 19, 2009) <http://successcircuit.com/maslows-hierarchy-of-needs>

Langlinais, CPA, Scott. *"Reducing the Opportunity to Commit Fraud."* (March 2008) <http://www.irmi.com/expert/articles/2008/langlinais03.aspx>

Lerma, A. *"Profile of a Con Artist."* Icarus Rising, Articles. (April 1, 2008) <http://earthbornicarus.wordpress.com>

Lloyd, J. & Mitchinson, J. *The Book of General Ignorance. Faber & Faber* (2006)

Logan, L. *"The Secrets of Stealth."* Wayofninja.com (October 2010) <wayofninja.com>

Madison, David. *"Tapping Individual Donors: A Strategy For Long-Term Financial Health."* Namac.org (April 2011) < http://www.namac.org/node/1214>

Mayo Clinic Staff. *"Diagnosing Alzheimer's: An interview with a Mayo Clinic Specialist."* MayoClinic.com. (May 2010) <http://www.mayoclinic.com/health/alzheimers/AZ00017>

Newman, Graeme R. & McNally, Megan M. *"Identity Theft Literature Review."* Reported to the Department of Justice, Contract #2005-TO-008 (July 2005)

Plazak, Dan. *A Hole in the Ground with a Liar at the Top.* Salt Lake: *University of Utah Press.* (2006)

Sinclair, David. *The land that never was: Sir Gregor MacGregor and the most audacious fraud in history.* Da Capo Press (2004)

"Social Engineering." Search Security. Techtarget.com (April 2009) <http://searchsecurity.techtarget.com/definition/social-engineering>

Sun Tzu quote, Author, Goodreads.com (July 2011) <http://www.goodreads.com/author/quotes/1771.Sun_Tzu>

Verma, Mukul. *"Abundant Future, A conversation about the transfer of $41 trillion in wealth and, why you can't tell Donald Trump to give it up for good."* Currents, Q3, (2007)

Wahba, A; Bridgewell, L. *"Maslow reconsidered: A review of research on the need hierarchy theory."* Organizational Behavior and Human Performance, 15, 212-240 (1976)

Werner, Carrie A. *"The Older Population: 2010."* 2010 Census Briefs, *U.S. Census Bureau* (2010)

Wikipedia contributors. *"Self-justification."* Wikipedia, The Free Encyclopedia. Wikipedia, The Free Encyclopedia, 5 Jan. 2012. Web. 23 Feb. 2012.

Yogi Berra quotes, Quotes by Athletes, BrainyQuote.com (August 2011) <brainyquote.com>

ABOUT THE AUTHOR

PHILLIP C. LEMMONS IS A graduate of the University of Southern California and Southwestern University School of Law. He was admitted to the California State Bar in 1998, and has practiced extensively in the areas of wills, trusts, conservatorships, elder law and probate. He has handled hundreds of probate matters involving will, trust and conservatorship contests,  administration, and planning. He is an active member of the Estates and Trusts section of the California, Orange County and Los Angeles County Bar Associations. Mr. Lemmons is a highly regarded advocate, speaker and educator on events affecting generational wealth transfers.

A FINAL WORD FROM PHILLIP LEMMONS

I TRULY HOPE YOU ENJOYED reading this book on Stealing Home, A Con's Guide to Inheritance Theft, as much as I enjoyed the writing process.

My primary aim is to help people get their full inheritance by stopping financial scams perpetrated by cons.

If any amount of your inheritance is under attack or vulnerable to scams and you would like to know more about what to do from someone who has gotten results for hundreds of people just like you, contact me.

If after reading this book you want to work with someone that believes in doing things right, taking full accountability and backing it up with action that actually gets results, give me a call.

(800) 840-1998

WE ARE ALWAYS HERE FOR YOU